The Ear and the Voice

Dr. A. A. Tomatis

Translated by Roberta Prada and Pierre Sollier
Freely adapted, with kind permission of the author,
by Roberta Prada and Francis Keeping
Originally published as "L'Oreille et la Voix," by Dr. A. A. Tomatis,
Laffont Paris 1988

The Scarecrow Press, Inc.
Lanham, Maryland • Toronto • Oxford
2005

SCARECROW PRESS, INC.

Published in the United States of America
by Scarecrow Press, Inc.
A wholly owned subsidiary of
The Rowman & Littlefield Publishing Group, Inc.
4501 Forbes Boulevard, Suite 200, Lanham, Maryland 20706
www.scarecrowpress.com

PO Box 317
Oxford
OX2 9RU, UK

British Library Cataloguing in Publication Information Available

Library of Congress Cataloging-in-Publication Data

Tomatis, Alfred.
  [Oreille et la voix. English]
  The ear and the voice / A.A. Tomatis ; translated by Roberta Prada and Pierre Sollier ;
freely adapted, with kind permission of the author by Roberta Prada and Francis Keeping.
      p. cm.
  Includes bibliographical references and index.
  ISBN 0-8108-5137-7 (pbk. : alk. paper)
  1. Singing—Physiological aspects. 2. Voice—Physiological aspects. I. Prada, Roberta.
II. Title.

QP306.T6613 2005
612.7'8—dc22   2004021365

♾™ The paper used in this publication meets the minimum requirements
of American National Standard for Information Sciences—Permanence of
Paper for Printed Library Materials, ANSI/NISO Z39.48-1992.
Manufactured in the United States of America.

CONTENTS

Foreword   v
Preface   vii
To the Reader   ix
How to Use This Book   xiii
Acknowledgments   xi

Part I Some Reflections on Singing

  1   Treating the Voice   3
  2   Singing, the Source of Energy   5
  3   What is a Beautiful Voice?   11
  4   Singing and the Right Ear   21
  5   About Singers   27
  6   The Art of Singing   37

Part II How the Ear Works

  7   About Listening   43
  8   Anatomy and Physiology   45
  9   The Ear and the Nervous System   55
  10   The Ear's Control of the Voice   65

Part III Vocal Technique

  11   How to Sing   79
  12   Listening Posture: Ear and Body   83
  13   Bone Conduction   89
  14   Breathing   97
  15   Vowels   107
  16   Falsetto   115
  17   What is Needed to Sing Well?   121

iv   Contents

18   Conclusion   133

Selected Bibliography   137
Index   139
About the Authors   141

FOREWORD

My introduction to the work of Alfred Tomatis began when I fortunately happened to be seated in front of an old friend, Susan Dash, at the Academy of Music in Philadelphia. It was at this time that she told me that she had been studying with Alfred Tomatis and his work. A few days later, Paul Madaule's book *When Listening Comes Alive* arrived by mail. I was immediately taken with these ideas and knew that this was something that could be of great importance for singers and teachers of singing, and it had a special fascination for me. In 1997 I saw Tomatis himself at the International Congress of Voice Teachers conference in London. In 1998 I was able to experience two weeks at the marvelous Toronto Listening Centre with Paul Madaule and found the results to be transforming and illuminating. In 2002 I invited Paul to address the convention of the National Association of Teachers of Singing (NATS) and lead a listening workshop at the Westminster Choir College. Since then I have learned more from my associations with Roberta Prada, Francis Keeping, Francoise Nicoloff, Daniel Shigo, and others who are using the work in uniquely creative ways.

This translation and adaptation of *L'Oreille et la Voix* is an important contribution to our understanding of the Tomatis work and its value. The changes that I have observed in those who experience communicative and learning disabilities are remarkable. The information age is providing us with knowledge of the factors that affect the vocal mechanism and provides us with a solid foundation as we teach healthy singing and speech. Now Tomatis has provided us with the next step. It brings all of this information together and encourages us to remember that the larynx is an organ of reaction and that the attuned ear improves posture, encourages expressive tone quality, and refines vocal control. I do believe that "it is the ear that sings," and the concept of the ear as creative rather than passive has helped me to understand why voices sound as they do and why some students don't progress or perhaps even lose the joy of singing. The larger definition of the ear and of true listening by Tomatis has inspired me as I seek ways to make my teaching more efficient and effective.

I have found that Tomatis people are always eager to share their discoveries. This translation will certainly bring the work of Alfred Tomatis to a wider audience and create a deeper understanding of what it means to truly be a Listener and therefore a more alert participant in life and music.

Marvin Keenze
Professor of Voice and Pedagogy
The Westminster Choir College of Rider University
Princeton, New Jersey
April 2003

PREFACE

This book is dedicated to the memory of my father, Humberto Tomatis. He was the seventeenth child of a large family and inherited his voice from his father. My grandfather took every opportunity to sing to us from his extensive repertoire of songs from Piedmont. He had such an infectious enthusiasm that he would pull together an impromptu chorus, which he harmonized and energized with his rich, raw sound.

My father was a born artist. He made up his face and stepped into character as easily as he put on his shoes. During an opera season he moved between Nice, Rouen, Marseilles, Toulouse, and Paris, playing the Cardinal Brogni in *La Juive*, Mephistopheles in *La Damnation de Faust* by Berlioz or in the Gounod *Faust*, Gournemans in *Parsifal* or Balthazar in *La Favorite*, Marcel in *Les Huguenots*, Hagen in *Sigurd*. He had 110 operatic roles under his belt, which gave him a tremendous grasp of singing. He was in all respects an accomplished artist, conscientious, scrupulous and blessed by nature with an extraordinary low register.

As a matter of fact, a good part of my childhood was spent in the wings of opera houses all over France. It was a very exciting place from which to watch. Even now when I sit in the audience, I can imagine the flurry of excitement behind the curtain. Between 1924 and 1931, I had the opportunity to meet just about everyone in France involved in opera. I was fascinated by what happened on stage and in the orchestra, and I absorbed it as if by osmosis. The repertoire, singing, and every aspect of the lyric art held no secrets for me. After 1931, my studies made it necessary for me to remain in Paris, so I was mostly absent from the theater. Nevertheless, when vacations permitted, I would return to that bustling world behind the curtain.

My own brief and rather sheepish career in opera began at eighteen months of age, when my father, no doubt envisioning this as the beginning of my training for the stage, had me go on as a baby in Massenet's *Manon*. I screamed bloody murder and had to rush off stage. I made one more pitiful appearance at age four and a half in *Carmen*. Obviously I was not destined for the theater.

As a young man I studied medicine and chose ear, nose, and throat (ENT) as my specialty. My father was a great help to me in my vocation. My father's friends and colleagues became my patients as soon as I opened my office. For a time, I became one of the most fashionable singers' specialists in Paris. *Phoniatre* is the name given in France to an M.D. who takes care of people whose voices are sick.

After 1944, my work led me to spend a great deal of time among the same people I had so often seen in the wings of the opera house. Although I had some initial doubts about choosing phoniatrie over a classic ENT practice, I went in thinking I knew all about singers and their world. Fortunately, over the years I came to a deeper understanding of singing.

Thanks to my father this book is rich in anecdotes to lighten the way. I hope that these stories will infuse the chapters that follow with my father's warmth.

TO THE READER

The ear lies at the heart of human experience. Dr. Alfred A. Tomatis relates that the fetal ear responds to sound and uses the energy it receives from the sound wave to shape the developing nervous system and brain. The way we think and perceive could not be more intimately connected with the ear. We singers live through our ears, and for us it is gratifying to learn that singing is such an important source of well-being.

I came upon Dr. Tomatis by chance in a book of essays. I instantly decided to try the listening, and I got more than I expected. I discovered I was really an alto, I found a higher placement, and my sound has become richer and more complex. Francis Keeping, my friend and teacher, concurs and has seen important changes in others who have done this work with us.

Tomatis is one of the earliest pioneers in the field now known as psycho-acoustics. *L'Oreille et la Voix* is a classic, first published in 1987, and the most recent reference it contains dates from 1984. It summarizes what was known at the time in this field and combines what Tomatis himself believed to be true. By adapting it with his kind permission, we can bring his passionate reverence for the ear and voice and his brilliant insights into the nature of listening and singing to the English-speaking world. His beliefs and theories are timeless and, if anything, are now garnering more support than previously.

Every day more findings in the field of developmental neurology confirm that the ear is as important in learning as the eye—perhaps more so. Since the 1980s research related to the development, anatomy, physiology, and pathophysiology of the ear and the vestibulo-cochlear system has provided new information and raised more questions. We have added some updates as notes, and included a current bibliography.

Just around the time when Hi-Fi was the latest advance in sound reproduction and Sigmund Freud was the man of the hour, Tomatis's work led him to explain how the ear relates to the brain in singing, music making, and by extension to the creative process. His work as house doctor at the Paris Opera and resident ear, nose and throat doctor (ENT) at the aeronautics lab in Saclay, where the Concorde engine was being developed, put him in contact with two seemingly divergent groups of people whose voice problems were identical. He discovered that auditory fatigue was the common thread. In the case of the workers at the jet lab, the company was anxious to get to the bottom of these complaints. They were leading to costly early retirement caused by job-related hearing impairment, believed to be permanent.

With the opera singers, the auditory fatigue was created by poor vocal technique, for one thing. Fortunately when the auditory system is not physically damaged, function can be restored or even improved. Tomatis devised an entrainment consisting of listening to specially prepared music, fed through a device he invented, called the electronic ear. His technique exercises the ear's hammer/stirrup muscles that, according to the Tomatis analysis, influence the tone of every other flexor/extensor pair in the body. Basically he reawakened the muscles of the ear by constantly shifting the input to the ear, so that every few seconds the ears have to readjust to the direction and quality of the sound. If you have ever watched a cat's ears as it listens, you will know how deeply embedded this shifting must be in the nervous system. According to him, the effect of the alteration in muscle tone is generalized throughout the body, shifting posture and harmonizing the involuntary nervous system as well as muscular activity.

After experimenting with various composers, Tomatis concluded that Mozart's music was uniquely suited to his purpose. He chose passages from certain symphonies and violin concertos, rich in high harmonics, at a tempo of 120, free from heavy emotional content that leads to distracting internal dialog. This training is intensely energizing and he at times uses Gregorian chant to induce calm breathing and lower the heart rate.

By reinforcing the highs and adding a strong experience of bone conduction, he recreates the experience that every artist with a great technique gives himself when he performs. He mentions the rich harmonic shower found in the singing of both Caruso and Chaliapin, whose recordings he studied. What characterizes great singing apart from its beauty is the brilliance that the Italians call *squillo*.

One of his most important observations was that excellence in performance depends upon training the right ear to take control. It silences internal chatter, which is generated in the left ear. Bravura technique cannot coexist with running commentary. Neuropsychiatrist Richard Restak, in *Mozart's Brain and the Fighter Pilot*, and in *The New Brain* agrees. The repercussions of this training are enormous. Tomatis's first group of singers, actors, and musicians found that they were learning and memorizing more easily, feeling energized, and sleeping better. Some asked if he would try the technique with their children to see if it would improve their school work. It worked so well that he began to pursue this serendipitous discovery, creating applications addressing auditory processing, ADD, stress reduction, hearing loss (whether psychological or physical), loss of speech through head injury or stroke and help with autism, to name a few.

This is the twenty-first century, and the science of electronics has advanced exponentially since the techniques so brilliantly pioneered by Dr. Tomatis in the fifties. Audiophiles may prefer spectacular high-end analog, but digital technology and advances in the new field of psychoacoustics have allowed us to progress beyond the first electronic ears. Dr. Tomatis would be delighted at the innovations that are furthering his work. The complexity and expense of administering listening sessions has until recently prevented their popularization, but that is changing as I write.

We owe an enormous debt to the pioneering work of Dr. Tomatis. This book is for you, and with it I hope to deepen your pleasure in what is already yours, the gift of song.

R. P. New York City, 2003

HOW TO USE THIS BOOK

Each chapter of this book stands alone. You can read straight through, select any chapter. The purpose of this book is to discuss the principal role of the ear in listening, in dispensing energy to the nervous system and in controlling the act of singing, the alignments which are necessary for singing, bone conduction and its role in vocal quality and in ease of vocal production, and vowels, which are key to ease in singing.

This volume comes from my experiences as an ear, nose, and throat physician specializing in voice pathology. It summarizes the teachings of the audio-vocal seminars, which I have given over the years. Participants prepare to sing by becoming attuned to the cardinal role of the ear. They gain a deeper understanding of the act of singing, enabling them to incorporate the related proprioceptive sensations. Moreover, they sharpen their hearing, which is a fundamental prerequisite to excellence in listening.

The technical part contains many new concepts. I have sprinkled it with stories to hopefully make the necessary study of the ear, its multiple functions, and its interactions with the nervous system seem less tedious. I have kept references to anatomy and physiology schematic to make it accessible to a wider public. The theory of the three integrators presented here sheds light on these functions. Thinking of the integrators as building blocks of the nervous system helps us to understand the ear and the rest of the nervous system. An overview of some of the neurological aspects of singing has been included, because it is, in fact, the brain that does the singing.

This book is written for people who do not normally study neurology and from their point of view the material may seem complex. I have included simplified diagrams to help clarify the discussion. I have included a bibliography of works that discuss each of these subjects in depth.

If you want to try out some of the ideas about singing in this book, you will need a second pair of ears. Hopefully you will have a good teacher as your partner in discovery.

Note: We have included some more current references for readers interested in more contemporary concepts of the neuroanatomical and physiological underpinnings of the vestibulocochlear system.

ACKNOWLEDGMENTS

Now it is time for me to thank all those who have helped make this work possible: Pierre Sollier with whom I pondered long over the French. Francis Keeping, my teacher and friend experimented with me at the piano and discussed and edited part 3 on vocal technique with me point by point, worked on the illustrations, observed my progress and that of others, and did the listening himself. My gratitude also goes to Dr. Tomatis, who was so gracious to us as we worked; to Lena Tomatis for her continued support; to Paul Madaule for introducing me to Marvin Keenze, whose appreciation for Tomatis and respect for this book got it published; to Chris Faddick of BigBangSoundworks, with whom I clarified many points about this work, and who is creating an affordable machine which will put this technology in the hands of anyone who wants it; Dr. Steve Rothstein for reading the manuscript early on and giving it his blessing. I also thank Tony Schulte; the late Jeremiah Gutman, Esq.; Jan Gerritsen; Astrid Webster; Dr. Dave Anderson of SETI Home; Stephen Josephs; Matthew Lewis, PhD; Giada Liscia Garrison; Shirlee Emmons; Maestro Raffaello Sapere; Johannis Loldrup; Dr. Lisa Danzig; Jamie Titus; Francesca and John Prada; Joshua Leeds; Alexander Doman; Dr. Ron Minson; Kate Minson; Elizabeth Verrill; Beret Arcaya; Moshe Landsberg; Daniel Shigo; Julie Carter; Alain Zürcher of chanteur.net; Maestro Roberto Sbolci; neurosurgeon Dr. Armando Basso; Kay Hogan for the use of the posture drawings; Anna-Barbara Widjuja; Dr. David Goldsmith for extensive help in vetting all scientific aspects of the current book; Sheila Allen of Pediatric Therapeutics for enriching this book with current material on learning and developmental neurology, and for supplying the new bibliography; and Josh Ofrane, our computer guru. All of the above (listed more or less in historical order of their involvement in this project), lent an ear, gave suggestions, and asked great questions, some of them slogging through earlier versions of this manuscript, for which I shall always be grateful.

PART I

SOME REFLECTIONS ON SINGING

CHAPTER 1

TREATING THE VOICE

When I began my medical career, not much was known about the vocal mechanism. The way we treated singers, and our understanding of how the voice worked, was primitive. When I was first in practice, I used traditional methods of treatment. Before long I realized I knew very little about singing. All I had learned during my years beside my father and his friends suddenly turned out to have only yielded a superficial understanding of singing. What was the real meaning of such terms as "covering, singing in the mask, placing the voice on the palate, not pushing"?

Faced with my first singer patients it became clear that jargon wouldn't help. One of my father's friends, a leading baritone at the Paris Opera had an apparently good technique and was an excellent interpreter. However, he started to sing off pitch in the high medium range and the higher he went, the flatter he sang. Accurate pitch was a parameter not much talked about in those days. Although I later had to revise my understanding of good vocal production, I believed then that I knew what was involved. But where in the body would one go to correct faulty pitch? It is possible to attain a high degree of technical proficiency without improving pitch sense. This paradox became my first subject of inquiry thanks to my father's friend. He was so accomplished and his interpretations were so compelling that his weakness was less noticeable to the audience.

He enjoyed a highly successful career but the pitch problem was a matter of self-respect. Wherever he sang he sought out leading specialists, desperate for a solution. In Vienna, he consulted with the famous Froeschels, considered the top man in the field, who later moved to New York City. According to Froeschels his larynx was hypotonic: his vocal cords were distended—too slack to sing on pitch, as though they were the strings of a violin in need of tuning.

Back then it would have been unthinkable for a neophyte to second-guess the diagnosis of an eminent physician. So when I examined this well-studied larynx, I obediently saw it as hypotonic and obediently carried out Froeschels's prescription by administering strychnine sulfate to his cords. Nothing happened! As the days passed, I started to increase the dose, driven by the singer's obsession. It was a tough case and not a great way to begin my practice.

For two years, every two or three days, I dealt with the man and became more and more frustrated. I kept increasing the dosages of strychnine until finally his vocal cords became so tight that they snapped shut. On stage, his voice cracked and he choked every time he opened his mouth to sing. Some success! His larynx had gone from hypotonic to hypertonic. Interestingly, throughout all this, he still sang flat!

Thanks to his persistence I began an inquiry that occupied the greater part of my life as a researcher. As a rule anyone can sing unless a rare organic condition prevents it. Whether or not someone sings beautifully will depend on the basic instrument, technical accomplishment, and musical talent, all of which depend on the quality of listening. The ear and the voice are intimately connected. In their relationship we can find answers to many questions.

CHAPTER 2

SINGING, THE SOURCE OF ENERGY

Although we lavish a good deal of attention on how to sing, we seldom ask whether singing arises out of a profound need, or whether it is simply one mode of expression among many others. It seems to me that man sings by instinct and the ability to intone must have come before spoken language. Language has rhythms, nuances, inflections, and timber, exactly like music.

The Cortical Recharge

What does singing do for us? It recharges the brain with energy, although we cannot yet define its nature. The brain is an exceptional organ in many respects. Modern science does not fully understand its mechanisms and perhaps it will always remain somewhat of a mystery. We think of energy as something you expend in activity, or we believe we feel it circulate in us, something like electricity. Some say it descends, while others say it rises. For some it is a fluid circulating through the body. Others feel it localized at "focal" points or chakras. The perception of energy is quite subjective. Some people feel "flows of energy" that fill them with mental and physical vitality. When we are feeling fine, we sometimes like to sing; and if we do, the more we sing, the more energy we get, and the better we feel. What I have just described is a feedback loop, or cybernetic circuit. The activity feeds itself, and enhances the mental and physical state brought about by singing.

As we describe the vocal techniques and organs that contribute to phonation, you will see that it is the brain, activated by the ear, which does the singing. The brain is made up of a multitude of cells—more than 15 billion have been counted to date. This extraordinary complex of cells uses energy to maintain many of its functions, notably the ones that support the diffusion of neuromuscular and neurovegetative information. The cost of maintaining the good functioning of such a complex organ is high. Blood circulation supplies nutritional maintenance in the form of glucose and the considerable amount of oxygen that makes the metabolic combustion possible. To go beyond that, the brain needs the kind of energy it can get from singing.

5

In order for the brain to think and be creative, it needs to receive a great deal of stimulation or energy, in the sense that it gives rise to physical-chemical processes at the cellular level, which result in nerve impulses that are measurable and give rise to an electrical field. We know that the brain needs to receive 3.5 million stimulations per second for at least 4.5 hours per day in order to function properly, and be alert and attentive. Otherwise you will experience feeling dopey and distracted. This energy can be measured as electricity, which proves that some phenomenon is taking place. But the goal is certainly not to produce electricity. If we could artificially provide the brain with the same kind of electrical power that it already produces on its own, this would not boost its potential and might even damage it. Singing stimulates the brain in a way that it welcomes, so that it thrives.

The organ of Corti in the ear is the organ of perception. In the zone of the lows there are only a few dozen cells, in the middle a few hundred, and in the zone of the highs, 24,000 cells await recharging. You can see that sounds predominant in lows have few receptors and this causes the brain to lose energy.

What is stimulation? Many points on the body prickle as a result of sound. Both the inside and the outside of the body are excited by its myriad of tiny pressures. In fact, when we ourselves sing there is an even stronger internal sensory response from mucous membranes, including the intestines, than there is to sound coming from the outside, on the skin.

That's not all. The ear coordinates all the other perceptions like the conductor of an orchestra, assembling and directing the many stimuli upon us into patterns that we can accurately perceive. Then it sends nerve impulses to the brain through its own distribution network. We live literally bombarded by a myriad of stimuli. We are constantly surrounded and imprinted by the activity of molecular fields in the air, which make up atmospheric pressure. This molecular bombardment helps shape our apparent physical structure and makes it possible for us to equalize external pressures whose minuscule stimuli go unrecognized by our conscious minds.

Singing is one of the most efficient ways to shape our body. Those with sensitive skin will perceive the subtle play of resonance more easily. So too, the thinner the skin, the more delicate the voice. Conversely, someone with a gruff voice often will have skin that is rough to the touch, especially on the hands, the arms, the face, and on the trunk—areas more richly supplied with sound receptors. The body literally vibrates with song and harmony. This gives humans a striking advantage in relating to the environment. The act of singing permits us to open a dialogue with space so that we become flooded by its vibrations and merge with it, acoustically speaking. As soon as you sing you get feedback from your surroundings. Does the sound drop with a dull thud, or does it spring back at you, and make you prick up your ears and feel cheerfully alive?

The Acoustics of Halls

Reverberation creates a rich harmonic bath that envelops both singer and audience and sends feedback between singer and hall. Some halls light up immediately and sing easily. Their liveliness inspires people to sing with great joy since their atmosphere invites, sustains, and activates the vocal gesture. These are characteristics of a great theater, a great concert hall. It is not easy to create such a space but happily a good many halls range from adequate to very good reverberation.

The singer does not always perform under ideal conditions. In difficult halls, he must adapt and accommodate just to keep himself together and give a decent performance. A singer can adapt up to a point, but the space must have some life. A completely dead hall does not permit singing and even extinguishes thought. Vibration disappears as if the walls had swallowed it; there is no reverberation, no sense of harmony with the surroundings. The result is a sense of desolation, of being out of balance, of suffocation. A good sonic return is a matter of primary importance to the singer.

Ideally a concert space should be able to vibrate and sing at the slightest excitation. The interactions between the singer's physical body and the acoustic environment create a proprioceptive image of the body, and they structure a sensory-motor experience of the surrounding space in a perpetual dialogue. We create the vibration and are in turn affected by the space we have set in motion. It is well known that the best halls inspire the best performances.

The Aesthetics of Sound

Since we are continually immersed in a sonic bath, good acoustics have the power to make us feel alive. It would be ideal if we could always inhabit spaces that enhance our aesthetic relationship to the acoustic environment. Some contemporary buildings have been constructed with that in mind. The Roy Thompson Theater in Toronto is an immense hall in which ambient acoustics can be shaped to suit the occasion. The number of musicians, the size of the audience and whether its members are lightly or heavily clad, all affect sound quality, as do humidity and temperature. In this hall, changes in the acoustics are electronically monitored and can be modified on the spot to suit specific conditions. In vibrant surroundings, we become alert to all of life's resonance and achieve a higher level of verbal expression. When architects create spaces consonant with the aesthetics of sound they support our creative impulses and provide us with much more than a sense of shelter.

Singing as a Function

Singing is a basic human function. It is a response to the need for self-expression and self-exploration. It creates body awareness and allows the singer to explore the environment through the impact on the body of returning sound. Even more important, it feeds and stimulates the nervous system. One need not be an accomplished singer for this feeding to occur. It is sad to think that people can feel inhibited throughout their lives because someone teased them when they were making their first attempts to sing. Please take every opportunity to sing. You will gradually improve. Of course there are exceptional people who immediately delight everyone around them, but we can all educate our ears to self-listening and singing. This is the best way to provide our nervous system with the high-quality stimulation that is indispensable to optimal functioning, even though we do not need to become opera singers to stimulate the brain's creativity.

Campagnola, Energy Restored

I once had the chance to treat Campagnola, a well-known singer at the time of Caruso. He was at his peak from 1910 to 1930. When he came to see me, he was 78 years old and he complained of having some difficulties in singing, a certain physical fatigue. I discovered that his ear had lost some of its potential and I decided he could benefit from a few sessions with the Electronic Ear. Campagnola was able to resume his activities, which were numerous. He spent all his time painting and singing for himself. He had absolutely enormous vitality. That is why he was so afraid of not being able to continue his activities with the same energy. As soon as he got his ear back in shape he became active again. You see that the loop is the same no matter what the age.

The Cantor

A fine tenor with professional fatigue came to me about twenty-five years ago. He was a lyric spinto with a long career in the opera. As a child, he studied the sacred chant of the synagogue and he was a consummate master of cantorial technique. Yet, he was so drawn to opera that he gave up the cantorate for the theater. I reeducated his way of listening and repaired the auditory wear and tear accumulated during his career. The intensity of his voice made everything in the room—the windows, and the crystal drops of the chandelier—vibrate. It took a strong ear to stand close by. His reeducation went so well that I mentioned him to the director of the Paris Opera, who immediately invited him to re-join the company. After several days the tenor told me that upon reflection, he had decided instead to leave immediately to help in the building of Israel.

I heard from him regularly. He told me that he would sing at full voice on the building sites where he worked as a construction foreman, in the open air, under the burning sun, to the glory of God. His synagogue was the whole of Israel. He had gone back to his roots. He reassumed his rightful place as the sacred singer he had been before he got sidetracked into the world of secular song!

Each time he visited France, he would return to my office for a "tune-up" before going back to the mission that filled him with such joy. He gave to others the most precious part of himself: a voice with the power to enchant. His song lightened the labor of others, increased their energy, invigorated them, and led them in perpetual prayer.

Recharging Function

It is interesting to see that both eastern and western ascetic practices designed to heighten awareness make use of the listening posture for meditation. That permits the brain to be charged with electric potential.

I love to tell the story of the adventures of certain Benedictine abbeys several years ago. After May 1968 in France, many customs were reevaluated and changes were made that did not always have the intended effect. Certain Benedictines decided that singing—in general the monks of these orders sing for six or eight hours a day—made them waste a lot of time, so they gave it up. They were tired all the time but they thought it was lack of sleep because they got up at night for offices. They started to sleep through the night and the more they slept the more tired they became. They looked elsewhere for the cause of their exhaustion. Perhaps their diet of mostly vegetables and occasional fish was causing it. They called in the Tremolinieres, nutritional specialists, who advised them to adopt a standard diet, which didn't help. So it was that one of the abbeys called me in.

When I arrived I found seventy monks out of ninety in their cells, completely exhausted, incapable of following the offices, not doing anything. As I knew the abbot well, I was able to persuade him to make his monks start singing again. And to help them wake themselves up, I left some electronic ears in the abbey. In a couple of months the abbey came back to life. Out of the seventy monks, sixty-eight of them got back their energy for thinking and singing. The abbot told me that the monks had begun bickering as well. When they resumed singing harmony in their relations was restored.

The singing posture is especially important to Tibetans in their ascetic practices. The high altitude of Tibet (4000 meters) poses them a problem because at that height, sound transmits less easily and the ear cannot function so well in the rich part of the highs. The sounds they emit are low, and for them to be charging in nature, the Tibetans must have many high harmonics. That is why the Tibetans spend so much time in the listening posture during meditation. They can thus emit "om" or "aum" making the low sounds (their larynxes cannot do otherwise at that altitude) at the same time that they create the highs. What is more, to augment the cortical charge, they have created an environment permanently alive with sounds of every kind, especially bells and little wind chimes, giving that tinkling sound that evokes the atmosphere of the Tibetan world.

Their famous OM is a charging sound only if it is well executed. It can be just as destructive as bad music when it is pronounced incorrectly. I have seen many people in my center in Paris who have thrown themselves into saying OM or repeating a mantra, but they do it in such a way that it leaves them completely empty of energy, regardless of the symbolic content. If the sound is of bad quality, it follows that the posture is incorrect and listening is faulty.

For some people OM contains all the letters of the alphabet in Sanskrit, A being the first letter and M being the last. That is one of the reasons for thinking that all sounds are contained in this one sound. In fact a lot does happen when you pronounce it right. It is a true charging sound. It begins with an open sound—"A," followed by a "U," and ends with a closed sound "M," which is closest to the bone vibration heard by the right ear.

At the time of Vatican II, when the church began to use the vernacular in liturgical chant, the Cistercians and Benedictines of Europe thought they would try their hand at Tibetan chanting. The lamas who came to visit our monks did not have the impact they had hoped. The lamas are prepared to utter their AUM at the top of the Himalayas and the Benedictines to sing Gregorian chant in their occidental abbeys. One cannot exchange with impunity religious chants adapted to the culture and place of their practice. This is a question of acoustic adaptation to place, a question of impedance. In fact AUM is not the only sound emitted by the Tibetans. They use six sounds, one for each of the chakras. Starting from the lowest, the sounds ascend with each chakra. And if you don't sound them properly, you would be better off taking a cup of tea instead.

Clearly singing is important. It energizes the singer as well as the listener. It has been scientifically proven that the brain, in order to operate at full capacity, needs to be bombarded with a great number of stimuli for several hours a day. Sound energy, transmitted through the audio-vocal circuit, makes an important contribution to peak functioning. We can never sing too much, any more than we can listen to music too often. It is critical, however, to clarify which kind of music and singing nurtures us.

CHAPTER 3

WHAT IS A BEAUTIFUL VOICE?

To say that a voice is beautiful because we find it pleasing doesn't tell us much. How is it that people can have such vastly different reactions to voices? Some of us will adore a certain singer while others can dislike the very same sound. If the objective of beautiful singing is to create a mutual experience of resonance between singer and listener, we need to know how that happens.

About thirty years ago, I treated a star of the lyric stage, reputed internationally to be one of the all-time great singers. He no longer sang, having lost his voice prematurely at the age of thirty-six. The reason for the unfortunate interruption of his career was hotly debated. People variously blamed his health, his technique, the way he lived, whatever they imagined. Yet, his recordings were something else. He had left us a wide repertoire of arias and I have yet to find anyone in artistic circles who failed to fall in love with that voice.

The means for exploiting a privileged instrument are always technical. If young singers have beautiful voices, they believe themselves to be good singers, particularly when audiences and sometimes even their teachers reinforce that notion. However, little by little, any difficulty they may have with technique will grow and become magnified, and singers will begin to feel the pinch, even though they continue to be invited to sing because their basic vocal quality is still good.

We have to detach from the beauty of a voice if we want to appreciate technique. We all know something about the performance of a professional, even one blessed with exceptional vocal qualities, because we feel his performance in our bodies. A professional singer with a great technique causes us to breathe fully, our pharynx opens, our larynx moves without tightening. The articulation is supple, passing from one syllable to another without breaking the melodic line, without losing intensity, and we are transported. With the inexperienced singer of poor vocal quality we can easily detect his technical weaknesses because we feel them.

On the other hand, it is possible to become so confused by a striking voice that we do not notice underlying technical faults. But whatever the initial success of such a singer, sooner or later he will lose his voice, and to our ears, often quite suddenly. This alone proves that he had a defective vocal technique. Since the larynx is a particularly solidly built organ, to damage it to the point where singing is no longer possible, the singer must subject it to especially rough handling; when that happens his speaking voice will also be noticeably affected.

Returning to our exceptional artist whose career had been prematurely interrupted despite his gifts: his technique undermined rather than sustained his vocal ability. By the age of thirty, his voice became less and less secure and he began to panic on stage. I remember seeing him in the wings, shaking like a leaf and hanging on to a piece of scenery, which began to tremble along with him. A large audience had come to hear his beautiful voice. Only he knew what it cost him to satisfy his public. Audiences ready to applaud his success were just as quick to react to his slightest flaw.

Twenty years later, when I had become a specialist in treating the voice, he came to consult me as he had countless of my colleagues. He had difficulty speaking. His voice was cracked, hoarse, and lowered in pitch. His larynx suffered from extreme tension, and was difficult to see because it had become hidden under pathologically distended false vocal cords. Although his last performance had been seventeen years earlier, his recordings still flooded the market. He was intensely homesick for the theater. Even if he could not perform on stage again, he still wanted to sing, if only to give examples, for he now taught singing to pass the time!

I asked him to record some phrases. It did not take long; in a halting, pushed voice, he tried to tame an Italian aria that he had loved to sing: "Un di al'azurro spazio" from *Andrea Chenier* by Giordano. He could only utter a few syllables, breathing in the middle of words, uttering an array of cracks starting on the first note in the high medium range, an F on the vowel e "…e sfolgorava d'oro." He stopped, out of breath after several measures, unable to finish the aria he had sung so often. It was clear his badly damaged ear had lost its control. An audiogram established that his hearing was very poor, damaged to the point of a kind of perceptual deafness that produced these ugly noises.

Singing badly causes sonic trauma, and eventually destroys one's ear. Sound trapped inside the head is loud enough to cause fatigue. When one sings well the sound is projected outward, and the ear perpetually monitors emission in order to control and to protect itself. Good technique protects the ear, which is the professional's means of vocal control. Good singing keeps the ear intact and preserves the quality of the voice. It creates a loop: one sings even better when one sings well; conversely, one destroys one's voice by singing badly. In the case of this singer, the feedback loop became a debilitating downward spiral.

Analysis of the Voice

What constitutes a beautiful voice? Using equipment to analyze sound by breaking it into its various component frequencies, we find an acoustic object that is characterized by volume, shape, and color. Frequency corresponds to the number of vibrations per second, which determines pitch. A note takes the name *do, mi* or *la* from its first formant. As pitch remains constant, volume modifies the intensity of the sound. Color is related to the presence of additional frequencies. A wide spectrum of variable harmonics is associated with the formants. The sound resulting from the relative intensities of added harmonics can be more or less colored, more or less brilliant, more or less dark or bright. It will be harmonious or inharmonious, and it takes on colors which we associate with emotions.

Our appreciation of a sound and its qualities depends on these three parameters: volume, shape, and color. We cannot ignore the setting that surrounds the sound. Generally, in music or singing, every sound is part of a whole. It is difficult to isolate sound, to analyze it or judge its qualities without taking into account the environment and the context in which it evolves.

Electronics, by isolating sound, makes it possible for us to hear pure sounds composed of a single frequency, with more or less intensity. They have form and volume but are completely devoid of color. Fundamental frequencies on any pitch do not have great quality. The ear has a poor physiological response to pure sounds; it loves complexity. In order for the ear to respond tangibly, a minimum of three frequencies must be put into simultaneous play; without them, there can be no discussion of esthetic quality. Repeated analysis shows that a sound of good quality, whatever its appearance, is a sound which is rich in harmonics that complement the pitch of the generating frequency, or first formant.

We are generally attracted to the color of the sonority and often base our judgment on that characteristic, rather than on the pitch. Nevertheless, the appreciation of quality is very subjective and individual. Some people prefer one voice to another or the color we associate with Italian, German, Russian or French emission, just as people prefer one instrument to another. We form our aesthetic judgment of the voice, especially the singing voice, based on the richness of frequencies associated with the fundamental.

In this discussion, we will limit ourselves to a voice that sings without a microphone. With the classical technique the artist finds the amplification of his voice by knowing how to effortlessly exploit the acoustics of the hall. Technically speaking, the entire art of singing consists of using the ear to adapt to the ambient acoustics, to the impedance of the surroundings. The singer must know how to detect the minimum resistance in the surroundings and discover its resonance to fully exploit these qualities in the course of performance. It is an entirely different matter to fill a hall with the voice alone than it is to flood the room through the miracle of electronics. The two cannot be compared.

The Star

As for our artist, the veteran sidelined after his moment of glory, more important than discovering that his ears were damaged was finding a way to help him get his voice back. My goal was to put his audio-vocal circuit back on track. It was a great responsibility given his reputation, and a challenge to the staunch conviction of certain specialists that little could be done in cases of professional deafness. As long as the only difficulty is functional and the organ is sound, full function can be restored. So I had every reason to believe that all was not lost.

With his consent, we began auditory reeducation using acoustic filters, concentrating on the areas of perception that had disappeared. At that time, all things electronic were a great novelty and it was an adventure for our star to embark on such a course of action. He was adaptable and cooperative. It was an adventure for both of us. We made a deal to meet almost daily. The "Tomato," my father's nickname, came up frequently in conversation, and the fact that they had worked together many times contributed to our good rapport.

I built a filter able to restore his ability to listen to himself as before, and to control his voice, using his records as a guide. After determining the frequency spectrum of his voice, I could pinpoint the way he controlled it during the first years of his career and enhance it. This was done with such precision that after several days he was able to control his voice as he had done some twenty years earlier. The electronic equipment into which he sang at half-voice was composed of a microphone, an amplifier, and a set of filters. It restored a fuller spectrum of overtones to his fundamental frequencies. (More about that in a minute.) Through headphones, his own voice was sent back to him as he sang. The same equipment with a different setting reproduced his habitual hearing when he was not speaking or singing.

He soon experienced an important change in his level of vocal energy and was able to produce musical phrases and even whole pieces, including some that had been part of his lyric past. Although his singing didn't recover its former lightness, it acquired exceptional power. After several weeks, he was able to return to the Opera, for a time...

Alas, his belief that he could already make do with only his own ears was premature. He would have needed to have continued his audio-vocal training for a good deal longer in order to nail it. But he thought that he had already mastered the auto-control of his voice. It was still precarious and could not be sustained unaided for very long without his continued reeducation. But it is difficult to convince someone who has experienced the revival of his voice that his ears should get the credit. He returned to his former unhappy state in a very short time.

The Painter Who Sang

Two other adventures with the same artist are worth recounting. Around the time I had built these special filters and he had been visiting my office for a while, I started to treat an Italian painter who was about twenty years old. He came with a long history of problems in his right ear, an old intractable chronic otitis that had begun to cause serious trouble. He was suffering from a pathological condition called cholesteatoma that needed surgery. Before operating, I needed an X-ray to assess the wear and tear, and an auditory assessment of the inner ear. The latter would determine the surgical approach. If the inner ear were involved I would have to remove the bones of the labyrinth. If, however, the inner ear were still functioning, I would need to sculpt around it to excise the pathological tissue, maintaining the integrity of the bony labyrinth as much as possible to preserve its activity.

The labyrinth still worked, and I was surprised to find his hearing functional but quite atypical. His curve favored high frequencies at the expense of lows. This relative anomaly was striking because it was identical to a curve I had been working on for some time: that of Caruso's ear. I discovered the identical auditory response curve in the right ear of my young Italian patient, a painter who had never, till now dreamed of singing.

If my hypothesis of right ear control was valid, this young man should have been able to sing easily; and with a Caruso-type sound. I figured out a way to get him to learn a couple of phrases so that I could record them. To my surprise, I heard that same kind of brilliant Italianate sound that characterized Caruso's voice.

I was so fired up that I wanted the professional participants in this research to share in my discovery. First I played the tape for the famous singer described above. Excitedly explaining what I had just done, I told him something of my patient's history and then let him hear the recording of the young Italian painter with its gorgeous quality and startling high notes. With a serious, almost pitying air, he told me that the young man sang like a—well, never mind what he said. That aroused my curiosity. Remembering how he perceived sounds, it occurred to me to play him the Caruso recording that I had especially worked on. It was the 1916 recording "a la paterna mano" from *Macbeth*.

As soon as it started to play, the famous tenor started to pace back and forth in my large office, incredibly agitated. He had never been able to understand how a voice so ugly, so hoarse, so empty, so dark, so caught in the throat, could have had such world-wide success. It was such an unusual reaction that it made me wonder.

Had there been a rivalry between them I could have understood, but my friend was such an amiable fellow. There had to be another reason. As soon as he left, I assembled a group of filters that allowed me to simulate his current state of listening and played a Caruso recording. It had become unbearable to hear! As for the recording of my young Italian patient singing so freshly, the sound was completely distorted. Now I understood why my friend had tried to temper my enthusiasm.

Two more things: First, Caruso's unconditional antagonist had been, without being aware of it, reeducated thanks to my work on the ear of Caruso! Had he been able to sing again at the opera, it would have been through technology that allowed me to superimpose reinforced highs on his own, to enrich his overtones. His own emission, limited to 1500 Hertz and too poor to sustain audiovocal synergy, was well below the high range of Caruso's voice and didn't have enough high frequencies to stimulate reactivation on its own.

Second, I had the hearing curve of the celebrated singer and also that of the young Italian painter. After surgery, he had retained his Caruso-like sound profile, leading him, quite naturally, to sing. I asked the tenor to give the young fellow some lessons in vocal technique. Their listening curves being opposite, I had a pretty good idea of what was going to happen, so I planned to keep an eye on them. In three or four lessons it became clear that they were completely in-compatible. The young man lost his voice for several weeks! After reeducating him, I advised him to sing in future with only his own ear and he was just fine. This combination of student and teacher is a crystal-clear example of what it means to be on different wavelengths.

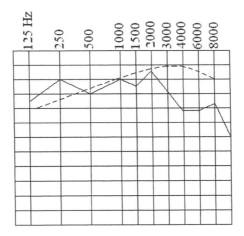

Figure 3.1 Comparison Auditory response curves of two
protagonists:
_____ Teacher,   ------- Student

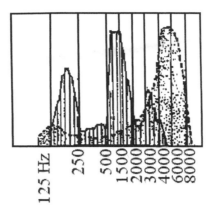

Figure 3.2 Voice curve comparison
------Voice of Caruso,   —Voice of French Singer

An analysis of Caruso's voice, superimposed with the spectrogram of the French artist and the voice of our rebellious singer makes an interesting comparison. (Fig. 3.2)Remember that despite the exceptional quality of his voice, the Frenchman's technique was so defective that it had completely obscured his vocal potential. A spectrogram of Caruso's voice has been added to complete this illustration and make it more intelligible.

The Singing Teacher

While the previous example may appear to be extreme, it is unfortunately not exceptional. The student and teacher must be attuned or the student is at risk. Being a good teacher depends on having a fine ear, and the best test of this is the teacher's own singing. Given an excellent technique, we can assume the teacher's ear is good enough. A teacher needs to have an exceptional understanding of emission. An exceptional voice is not required.

For a singer, virtuosity means neurological control of those parts of the body specialized in singing, as if it were a musical instrument. To learn this, a student needs an expert teacher with a talent for demonstrating proprioceptive sensations, which the student needs to discover in his own body. To truly know a subject, the teacher must have experienced it in his own body before he takes on the enormous responsibility of teaching. He must give the student the means to master the art of singing and guide him towards self-discovery.

The good execution of a musical piece demands that the nervous system and the body memorize the piece. This is true whether the vehicle is a musical instrument or the body using the medium of language, as is the case with a singer or an actor. Having learned to merge himself with his instrument, the great virtuoso can then become totally objective at will. This permits him to enter into the spirit of the music in the same way that the composer did as he wrote the piece. The violinist is a good visual example of both the fusion and the objectivity at work.

Some teachers unfortunately do not deserve their glowing reputations but owe them instead to the luck of teaching students who are naturally gifted and already have perfect audio-vocal control. A teacher with twenty students, ten of whom are successful, is a fine teacher. If a teacher has only two good pupils he is just lucky.

One of the most famous teachers in Paris owed his prolonged celebrity to just one student, who rose from the chorus of the Opera to become a principal singer because of her exceptional mezzo voice. Her maestro believed that he had created her and that he was a great teacher, but she would have made a career no matter what. Thanks to her, he was all the rage for a while. Having a famous star as a student allowed this bum to reach a much wider audience than he deserved. His favorite student was impervious, because she was strong as an ox, but he did harm others. This screwball believed the secret to singing was breathing from the gut, actually from the sex organs. A good part of his teaching consisted of squashing the student with a heavy pile of scores on the belly as he lay on the floor and then forcing him to sing. For high notes he would deliver a well-placed kick in the butt to the unhappy singer, now standing. Truly amazing!

Alas, such charlatans are far too numerous. Many are not quite as extreme but are no less dangerous. One teacher based his instruction mainly on laryngeal support, bringing on enormous tension in the vocal cords. His students regularly strangled and he, when he decided to demonstrate, would stop, pretending to be overcome with emotion. He could not tell them that he was, in fact, in the grip of a laryngeal spasm so severe that it made him wheeze. Yet, even he had his hour of glory. Despite singing as badly as he taught, nature had given his voice a beautiful natural color.

It is possible to get pleasing sounds out of an instrument without knowing how to use it. Beauty of sound fills many hopefuls with illusions about their prospects. Only a practiced ear can tell whether a singer is headed for trouble. Sometimes those who are not gifted with a beautiful voice have a better chance for a career. They know they have to work. Of course, they will need a good teacher and those are rare. You will have to search carefully to find one who is right for you. Once you have a teacher it will be he who will need good judgment.

I used to think a beautiful voice and excellent technique were all that it took to make a good singer but experience has taught me otherwise. Singers of every kind—French and foreign, lyric and others—have passed through this office. First I restructure their auditory potential and awaken the controls necessary for listening. Second, there is a period of practice to solidify the sensations that are awakened as the result of excellent hearing. Both are achieved through the use of the Electronic Ear.

Every evening between 8:00PM and 11:00PM for twenty years, I held seminars that led singers to become conscious of their proprioceptive sensations. As soon as they did, I knew they no longer needed my help to access the mechanisms leading to the control of the voice. This gave me great practical experience in training singers.

An Exceptional Jewel

In the course of these classes, I discovered a soprano who had a voice that went from a rich low to a brilliant and colorful high, as well as a flawless technique. The most fantastically embellished score held no obstacle for her. She was marvelous to hear and we believed that her future was assured, but she never made it. While everyone else left to begin a career, our exceptional nightingale stayed in class. For two or three years my wife and I had still hoped to launch her. But we had overlooked one thing. Our protégé was not an artist. Her technique was an example to everyone who came to work with us, but her delivery was vapid. She was serious and courageous but she was unable to make art.

The Virtuoso

A fine artist can transport us without a beautiful voice. I still remember Victor Forti, a baritone, with a wooly voice. Despite his great artistic and musical qualities, his career as a baritone at the *Opera Comique* was a failure. But he found a venue for his abundant intelligence and musicality. With Wagner he moved higher and became a Heldentenor, his voice still devoid of brilliance.

Forti was singing *Tannhauser* in Marseilles in about 1930 when I first heard him, having taken over the part from Georges Thill. His first act was difficult, without applause, and intermittent catcalls marked the discontent of the audience. As the evening continued he won them over and in the last act he was greeted with wild enthusiasm.

This man knew his Wagner. When he sang he became the music. Even though every show began with a difficult launch, it always ended in wild applause and many curtain calls; such was his ability to move an audience. He was an Italian Jew whose family came from Tunisia, and WWII unfortunately ended his career.

CHAPTER 4

SINGING AND THE RIGHT EAR

Forty years of experience have taught me that we sing with the ear, specifically with the right ear. It has been a long time since this idea crystallized, bidding me to solve the riddle of that famous singer with pitch problems.

Knowing that we sing with the right ear serves to deepen our understanding. Whether we look at singing through the use of the resonators or via a deep study of breathing, or by discovering the different supports for the registers or tessitura, etc., we are talking about neurophysiologic dynamics. It is true that without mastering the breath one cannot sing; but it is possible to know all about placement and still not make a decent sound.

To sing, the brain draws on systems of control centralized in the cerebral cortex. The organs of control are those which function during a specific activity. For example, the eye controls the acts of drawing, painting, and writing. In the very complex act of writing, the ear also plays a part. The letters of the alphabet that make up written language are visual representations of sounds. They have to be vocalized internally to come alive, to be combined to make syllables, words, and full sentences. The same is true for musical notation; it is a symbol for the note it expresses.

So, while the eye controls the movement of the hand as well as most other movement, the ear controls listening. The ear is an organ of remarkable potential that does not just regulate the listening process but also intervenes in other human activities. We are generally aware of only a few more obvious functions of the ear. Some of its functions—hearing, balance, posture, gait, and the movement of all parts of the body—may seem to be unrelated. The ear is altogether different from other sensory organs: the nose, the skin, or even the eye. Its role is so enormous that we still have much to learn about the way in which it controls our lives. When he decides to put the entire nervous system at the disposal of the ear, man becomes a receiver.

This will to attend is more pronounced when we listen to ourselves speaking than it sometimes is when we listen to others. With singing, the need to attend is even greater. The singer must focus on each sound to give it pitch, color, and inflection while simultaneously adding intention and articulation. This is the essence of control: to make sure that nothing passes without strict verification.

However, these are only a few of the parameters that the ear must master in singing. Happily, these controls do become habits, so when the ear is ready all the mechanisms of singing will fall readily into place, leaving the singer free to make music and interpret.

If the right ear is not ready to assume control, no amount of study will produce a dependable enough technique to give the singer the freedom to sing beautifully. We make sense of what the singer transmits to us through experiencing his body sensations reflected in our own. We can tell in our gut when we hear good singing, and our negative reaction is an automatic self-protective response to bad singing. Most of the time we find singing that is more or less okay and we have a good time at the theater mostly because the music is beautiful. Occasionally we experience a virtuoso performance and its effect on us is unmistakable. We immediately know that most of what we have otherwise been hearing has been merely acceptable.

Many years ago, while trying to prove that the right ear is the director, I carried out certain experiments. The simplest one was to saturate the right ear with sound to see what would happen. Any singer who was subjected to this trial was immediately unable to control his voice. He thought that he was singing easily, as if he had been liberated. What had occurred, however, was that he became freed from his auto-control, just as if he were drunk. It was not a pretty thing to hear.

If you change the way a person listens with the right ear by filtering the sound you can take away anyone's ability to perform. If you alter zone one (125-750 Hz) he will sing on pitch but with poor quality. Changing how he hears in zone two (750-3000Hz) he will sing out of tune. Blocking zone three (greater than 3000) he will sing in tune but devoid of brilliance. You can do a little experiment. If you are right ear dominant and you block your right ear you will note that the sounds seem to be lower in pitch because, by blocking your right ear, you are forced to use the longer route of the left ear and lose some highs along the way. If blocking the right ear does not change the pitch, you have been using the left ear as the dominant. This can be altered by training. (From some reports there is an exception: people who flip-flop dominance. The ear you use to listen on the phone is not a good test, because people tend to leave the dominant hand free to write, so the phone would be on the nondominant ear.)

Saturation of the right ear is obtained by subjecting it to an intense sound for a very short period of time, 100 decibels for ten seconds, for example, as in tests for auditory fatigue. The time can be increased to twenty or thirty seconds without danger. The resulting phenomenon, called auditory saturation, affects the ear in the same way that a flash bulb will blind the eye for a few moments. It creates a negative image that leaves a persistent scotoma or hole until the macular cells recover. Functionally, it may not be exactly the same for the cilia cells of the cochlea as it is for the eye, though we cannot be sure. Maybe intense sound temporarily shuts down the physicochemical excitations taking place between dendrites of the afferent nerves leading to the central nervous system. In any case it leaves a sort of negative remnant and for a time overwhelms the control. The same test applied to the left ear has no effect and may even facilitate the flow of sounds by getting it out of the way of the right ear.

The Challenge of Michel Dens

Every singer with whom I have tried the saturation experiment has been thrown off for a few moments before recovering except for Michel Dens. He had a longer career than many of his colleagues. His energy was inexhaustible. Certainly, he sang well and we know that good emission is an energy-giving tonic. Nevertheless, it would seem that such a phenomenon should have limits. I was intensely curious to discover how he could be so resilient. I asked him to undergo the Peyser test for auditory fatigue capacity, subjecting the right ear to bursts of pure sounds of 2000 Hertz for thirty seconds.

Dens underwent this experiment with pleasure despite his heavy schedule. He had been performing every night in *The Land of Smiles* at the *Gaite Lyrique* for several weeks, while spending his afternoons making recordings at Pathe-Marconi, and on Tuesdays, his day off, he was making a film in Germany. Many of his contemporaries had seen him tour France by car performing daily or every other day, singing the whole baritone repertoire from the lightest to the heaviest. He was a star in such roles as *The Land of Smiles* and he also sang *Rigoletto* or *Herodiade* and could then switch to *Les Cloches de Corneville*. He was, in short, a phenomenon. (At this time he was singing both baritone and tenor roles. On my advice he later limited his singing to baritone roles.)

I believed that he was indefatigable essentially because his ear was exceptionally resilient. That is why he had perpetual control at his disposal. I was unable to discover his ear's limitations. I had gradually increased the time of saturation of pure sounds at 2000 Hertz beginning with thirty seconds and, for the first the first time in my life as an investigator, I did not see changes appear in audiometric control. I tried one minute, then two: still nothing. At ten minutes I called a halt, fearing that if I went any further I might create a permanent residual scotoma.

As we were saying good-bye, we decided that the day after his last performance of *The Land of Smiles*, we would spend the afternoon doing another endurance test. We had agreed to work on "Under the white shade of the apple trees in flower" from *The Land of Smiles*. He had been singing that song every day except Tuesday (on these days off, he was filming in Germany) at the *Gaite-Lyrique*. He sang six days a week, eight shows, all with encores. We figured out that he had sung the song around a thousand times. It was reasonable to assume that he had acquired automatic control over his emission in that piece.

This was the test: standing in front of a microphone and wearing headphones, Dens sang while he heard himself through an amplifier. Both ears heard his voice simultaneously. We made several trial runs to regulate the level of intensity being fed back to his ears. The results were recorded so I might analyze them more closely. In the first part of the experiment, auditory conditions were the same as during the show. The voice was brilliant, well modulated, supported, as always.

In the second part of the experiment I suppressed the auditory control of the left ear by altering the balance of the feedback. A recording of the aria showed us that by favoring the right ear, the directing ear, he gained still better control over his singing. The voice became suppler, lighter, more tinted, endowed with a more precise and marked articulation. It was incontestably better directed. In part three of the test, the right circuit was suppressed, making the left ear the pilot. The emission immediately became uncontrolled and sounded as if Dens had never sung before. He supported in an exaggerated manner, his voice went flat, lost pitch, and had difficulty ascending. In no time, we witnessed the dissolution of every habit of this vocal athlete.

For this finding alone, the experiment had very important implications. It confirmed the prime role of the right ear in the control of vocal emission. I repeated the experiment with many singers, including Beniamino Gigli, always with identical results. This test is easily reproduced but it must respect the auditory system. By using feedback of moderate intensity, I obtained the same results with instrumentalists.

The Stradivarius of Francescati

One day I had the good fortune to receive violinist Zino Francescati, which was an enormous windfall for me. When the violinist's right auditory circuit was experimentally blocked in favor of the left, his playing became totally disorganized. He said, "This is not me playing. There is nothing beautiful about it." Then he added, "If I had not seen for myself that it is my right ear that plays, I would have guessed that it was my left since that is the one that rests against my violin."

I had no doubt that the right ear was dominant, and that it acted as the directing ear. Etymologically, the word "directing" means "right." This directionality, confirmed by Francescati, was accompanied by other remarks that were significant from a research point of view. Experimenting with Francescati's right ear yielded the same findings as with singers, a modification of the quality. After introducing a filter at 1000 Hertz that only allows the low frequencies to be heard, his playing became heavy and thick. His bowing was different. His rich high palette disappeared along with his pitch control.

What especially drew my attention was a remark that Francescati made: "Not only does it affect my ear, but I can no longer move my fingers!" He was speaking of his left hand because he was no longer master of his right hand, which held the bow. When he could hear up to 1500 Hertz through the use of a higher filter, his Stradivarius developed a nasal sound, strident and weak. Francescati said, "My arm hurts and I have the impression that the violin is open, broken." One can entirely change the playing of a violinist by modifying right auditory control. There is nothing in the body that does not react, however

slight the intervention. That the nervous system responds totally to such modifications is now a well-established fact. Change in the right auditory system and
its accompanying integrators yields very specific, high order results.

The experience with Francescati led me, in the ensuing years, to elucidate
the neurological mechanisms underlying his reactions. It became evident that the
neurological processes at play in Francescati, as well as in the singers, could be
easily explained. But rethinking the neurology of the ear in order to arrive at a
unifying concept took up a good part of my research. Part II presents some of
my findings, especially those concerning the importance of the integrators.
These act as operational blocks at different levels that make it easier to study the
neuropsychophysiology of the nervous system. The right ear has a special role;
it coordinates phonation and all musical faculties and the left ear cannot replace
it.

The Exception: The Left Voice

I found my exception in an American baritone who had toured the world in re-
citals. He made a habit of stopping wherever he knew of a maestro who might
help him to improve his technique and interpretation. He performed often in
Paris and never lost an opportunity to study *melodie* with Bernac. I was always
invited to attend his concerts and had many occasions to examine him in my
office. Two observations resulted. First, he was left-handed and left-eared. That
meant you could see his face was more active on the left, and of course his entire pharyngeal dynamic and articulation were reversed. His voice lacked the
color that high harmonies give and was irritating. It was hard to move, affecting
his tempo, with a marked tendency to slow down. Secondly I noticed that the
same audience always attended his concerts. As I look back, it seems to me that
his loyal public may have consisted mainly of left-eared people, as they would
be most likely to enjoy his singing!

When testing for auditory saturation of his left ear, I realized that all rem-
nants of prior learning had disappeared. His right ear, which was wholly under
left auditory dominance, was incapable of taking the lead. The exception confirmed the rule that the left ear could never under any circumstances replace the
right. No matter how solidly educated and thus dominant, the left ear can never
completely assume the role of director.

What is true for singing and music is also true for language. The left ear is
capable of filling in but it can never take over that special role which is reserved
for the right ear—specifically, the regulator of all phonation, both vocal and
linguistic.

As we can see, in people who can hear, the ear is the principal force in this
work. We sing with our ear, speak with our ear, stand upright and walk thanks to
the ear. We perhaps even live thanks to our ear! This concept has two aspects:

1.   A simple aspect in the sense that everyone thinks he knows what we

mean by listening. In fact, the ability to listen is rare.

2.   A complex aspect in that we have not yet come to terms with true listening. When we listen, we are utterly changed.

Even with complete attention, it is a challenge to listen precisely to how we
say what we say so that others get the message we intend. Listening to ourselves
or to others requires a self-effacement that few can attain. The kind of listening
required in singing demands enormous self-discipline.

Is a Good Ear Enough to Make You a Good Singer?

No, of course not. A good ear is a necessity, but you must also want to sing, and
you still have to master the coordination of all the elements controlled by the
ear. The mechanisms of singing can often start operating spontaneously after the
ability to listen well has been cultivated. Then all the rest falls into place: posture, ample breathing, etc. Only the right ear is capable of organizing listening
and all that flows from it because stimuli from the left ear have to cross the corpus collosum in the brain and will lose time in conduction of impulses. Someone
with a good ear is seldom indifferent to music. But it takes time to get from simply singing to mastering the control of a musical phrase. For that you need not
only the ear, but intelligence and fire in the belly.

Note: Recent studies have demonstrated that control of music-making by
the right ear is extremely important for professional musicians. In addition, studies have indicated enhanced cerebral activity by musicians as compared to non-
musicians when playing or listening to music.

Many are very happy singing just for themselves, even without a perfect
ear. There are other cultures in which children still sing in school, and choral
singing is a popular pastime, one worth cultivating. Singing provides important
stimulation. It is one of the major means for recharging the brain. You can do it
anywhere. Certainly the brain is not concerned with esthetics, as long as it gets
recharged. The consequences for the nervous system of being deprived of such
healthy stimulation are dramatic. One can never sing too much. It is one of the
most complete modes of expression, involving mind, body, and emotions. When
fully expressed, it goes beyond charging the brain. One passes through different
states of consciousness to reach a higher level of mind-body integration.

CHAPTER 5

ABOUT SINGERS

Many years ago, I was fortunate enough to meet Beniamino Gigli. He was an exceptional artist whose marvelous technique allowed him to sing right to the end of his life. In the course of our conversation he compared his vocal color to a diamond, and that of Caruso to gold. We spoke about how Gigli controlled the shape of his vowels, how he made sure of his technique, and many other exciting things that utterly beguiled me. We talked about other singers, mainly the French. He made an interesting remark, especially considering the difference between how a Frenchman and an Italian hears. "I have noticed how many beautiful voices you have in France, but I have never understood why they all seem to sing an octave lower."

Gigli was speaking of the upper partials, which did not reach the Italian level of sonority. He had recognized something very important. The French ear is narrowly fixed between 1000 and 2000 Hertz, offering a rich frequency band at this level. The Italian ear goes much higher, to about 3000 Hz, giving the Italian voice its spontaneous brilliance so admired in singing. The French sound stopped an octave short. When he heard it, his proprioception was thrown off: breath, posture, placement of his sound, all the essentials of his singing.

Caruso: a giant among singers. He had an exceptional voice and he used it brilliantly with a vast range of shadings, during his almost twenty-year career. I learned a great deal about him through his friend, the tenor Campagnola, who always spoke of Caruso with great warmth and enthusiasm.

Enrico Caruso

Gigli's description of the golden color of Caruso's voice was apt, and we might well ask how this sound was achieved. Caruso had a sound all his own, no doubt related to the shape of his body and his massive face, and a powerfully developed thorax, 140 cm around with only 4.05 liters of moving air. These factors certainly contributed to his vocal quality, but they are secondary to his principal gift, an exceptional ability to listen to himself in order to control his voice. The development of his chest allowed him exceptional control over his breath.

Upon concluding that the larynx can only produce what the ear can hear, I became especially interested in Caruso's voice. This law, that one can only deliberately reproduce a sound that falls within the limits of self-monitoring, and the functioning of that feedback loop, has been repeatedly verified in the laboratory. It establishes a reciprocal action between audition and phonation so they exactly match one another. Since then, I have used my discovery extensively in education, reeducation, remedial teaching, etc. Vocal emission is controlled by the ear. It is easy to determine how a given singer hears by analyzing the frequencies that comprise his voice. I was able to demonstrate this between 1946 and 1947, when I built an analyzer with the help of an electronic engineer. Once I had visual representations of Caruso's long notes, I was gradually able to deduce how he heard his own voice. After completing a great number of these graphs, I was able track his listening. I could chart how he had continued to alter the response curve of his ear until the moment came when the quality of his voice had changed. It first grew larger, then it became organized in the mouth, and finally there was an alteration of the vowels.

From original master recordings, I was able to collect some very interesting research material regarding his emission. Despite the technical limitations of early recordings, the gorgeous cello quality that distinguished Caruso at the height of his powers shone through. For me, the flowing nature of its timber remains unequaled. I have never discovered in my analyses another voice so rich in frequencies nor so high in upper partials, even with all the advances in modern recording techniques. What Campagnola said could be verified: "No note ever uttered by another singer could make us forget the beauty of Caruso's voice."

Phonograms are visual representations, or graphs, obtained from a cathode ray tube that analyzes the frequencies of a sound from low to high, emphasizing the higher frequencies. It is interesting to note that in the spectrograms or phonograms of Caruso, the high range is quite distinct from the lows, with an almost complete absence of frequencies between 500 and 2000 Hz. Additionally, the slope of his hearing curve presents a drop of more than twelve decibels per octave starting at 2000 Hertz toward the lows, which is a considerable drop. Certain of the higher notes show a difference of eighteen decibels per octave. This is all the more remarkable because I have not found it in other singers. It is truly unique to the voice of Caruso. Since we know where control resides in singing, we can say that the phonograms reflected the responses of Caruso's right ear. From the recordings made between 1901 and 1914 we note that Caruso had an enormous energy: the shower of harmonics was between seven and fourteen times higher than the fundamental, as we can see in the following diagrams. The steep slope of the graphs leads us to conclude that Caruso's right ear was deaf to the transmission of low sounds!

Obviously you can sing well while being deaf to lows. I scoured the literature to find out what had happened to Caruso's hearing, but apart from his artistic life, little was known about him. In addition to Campagnola, I also met three other artists who had known him and had sung with him. All four told me that

Caruso always asked them to stand on his left side when they were talking because he heard badly from the right. The range of frequencies in conversation occupies the mid-range, lower than singing range. This fact further proves his deafness to low frequencies. His right auditory nerve only allowed him to hear the frequencies located in the zone required for singing. One might therefore attribute Caruso's singing to his inability to hear sounds of poor quality.

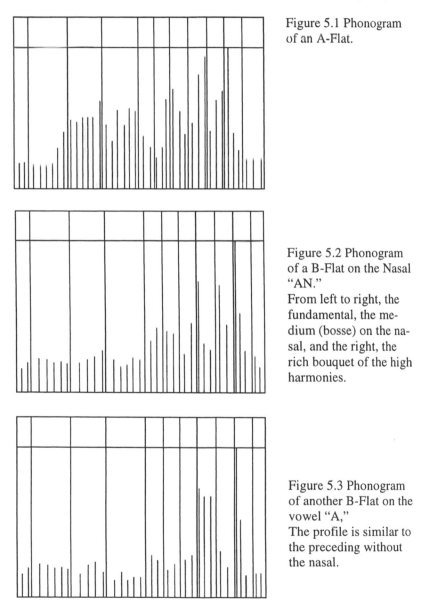

Figure 5.1 Phonogram of an A-Flat.

Figure 5.2 Phonogram of a B-Flat on the Nasal "AN."
From left to right, the fundamental, the medium (bosse) on the nasal, and the right, the rich bouquet of the high harmonies.

Figure 5.3 Phonogram of another B-Flat on the vowel "A,"
The profile is similar to the preceding without the nasal.

You can train your ear so that you hear yourself the same way that Caruso
did when he sang. When you have Caruso's kind of control in place, your singing will follow. You need only sing into the microphone with the headphones
and the filter that makes you hear your highs as Caruso did his. Your sound will
be yours because quality depends largely on anatomical factors. But you can
acquire a type of control which makes you keenly aware of high partials, and
that will give the opportunity to become a virtuoso.

Among other singers of stunning potential Chaliapin was a standout. His
voice had fully as great a harmonic shower at the top, with of course the addition
of a stunning low voice. A true bass will always have rich highs, as will many a
contralto. High voices are those that stop short of the bottom, those in the middle
(baritones, mezzos) add a strong part lower than tenors and sopranos. Basses and
altos add a strong bottom range. They have the widest ranges of all.

"But I Do Caruso's Exercises."

The fellow who said this came to my office laden with books of vocal exercises
attributed to Caruso! He could not fathom why he was having vocal problems.
He had been singing at the Opera-Comique for several years but had paralyzing
stage fright. He had that classic Italian sound, unfortunately messed up by his
training "in the French manner." He never acquired a well-integrated vocal technique. As long as he sang in private he was okay, but his high notes, though
powerful and brilliant, were unreliable. In performance he fell apart.

Although at first he sang baritone, he switched to tenor because he had a
beautiful, ringing top. But he never learned to manage the upper fifth properly.
He supported the same way on top as he did on the bottom, and so his larynx
was always in danger of flying up. The day after a bungled high note, topped off
by a huge crack, he came to see me because he had totally lost his voice. For the
first time, I saw a larynx completely inundated in blood. A hemorrhage under
the mucus membrane had suffused the whole vocal apparatus, which was extremely swollen. Silence and some local treatment would remedy this temporary
handicap. If he wanted to keep singing he would have had to change his technique, but he was too set in his ways. He washed out of the theater and luckily
he was able to fall back on his previous training as a sculptor.

The larynx is under the direction of the ear, which determines the sequence
of habits that make up singing. It is here that the conditions in the *passaggio* and
the changes in support are negotiated so that the larynx can operate without en-
gaging in dangerous activities.

According to our sculptor, the larynx was the sole cause of his problem and
that was the only part in need of care. I was obliged to deal with the acute state:
the effect, and never the cause. He rejected the opportunity to address the fundamental source of his troubles.

Of course, during the active phase of his career, Caruso's warm-up was to
try a few phrases, generally part of "A Vuchella," a Tosti song. He could tell

from those few notes whether or not he was in good voice. If the sculptor had known that, he would not have come to see me, weighed down by two briefcases bursting with exercises supposedly attributed to Caruso. (Caruso trained formally as a singer in both Naples and New York. During that time we know from his writings that he vocalized as assiduously as any other singing student must do, and that he had ten years of study and performance before he was even noticed.)

The way exercises are done is more important than the way they are chosen. Once he was fully launched as a professional, a single phrase was enough for Caruso. Gigli would test his voice with the first few bars of an aria from *L'Africaine* in Italian, "mi batte il cuor" or "m'appari" from *Martha.* Campagnola would find his voice in *Lakme* or *Les Pecheurs de Perles.* Essentially, the singer is checking to see how his ear is doing, although it seems as if he is testing the condition of his larynx. It was the ear that the sculptor lacked. Having a good instrument is not enough; you must also know how to sing. And that comes from knowing how to listen to yourself. If he could have listened to himself properly he would not have been wearing himself out with hours of vocalizing during the active phase of his career.

My Fair Lady

Here is a story that highlights the role of the larynx in singing. A great pop artist had lost his voice. The kind of hoarseness he displayed suggested important injuries to the larynx and I found an enormous polyp on one cord. It was necessary to remove it, but addressing the cause was the real goal since such damage comes from poor technique. I told my patient that after surgery his voice would require reeducation through the treatment of his ear. He had doubts about my advice and he got a second opinion from one of his compatriots, also an ENT specialist. This doctor was dismissive of my recommendation. Wasn't I "the ear nut? This idea was purely theoretical; better to ignore such nonsense!"

But clever words from my colleague could not give this tenor back his voice. He went from one specialist to another. Each one joined in rejecting my findings. In bouncing around from expert to expert, he finally landed in the office of Dr. Tarneaud, the unchallenged leader of the specialty in France. He knew about my research and sent the fellow back to me. Now he returned willingly. Several weeks had meanwhile passed, and our singer had been engaged as the very well-paid star of a French version of an American musical. I operated on him and reeducated him. He made a recording without difficulty and introduced the piece to Parisian audiences with great success. Since that time, roughly twenty-five years ago, he went on to make a career and returned from time to time to make sure his listening stayed in good shape.

How did he get into trouble in the first place? He had started his career with a natural voice and quality ear control which I restored after I operated on him. But the loss of his voice was the result of his decision to have plastic surgery. Be advised! Touching the face alters the dynamic interplay of all the facial muscles. This interferes with the neuro-muscular structure that is vital to singing. The face receives its entire motor innervation from the facial nerve, or seventh cranial pair, the same nerve that commands the stirrup in the middle ear. The muscle of the stirrup plays a predominant part in the regulation of the inner ear. Through it the ear exerts its control, which, in this case, had been lost. Without that regulation, the larynx sings however it can, that is to say, badly. That's what happened to this singer.

The same thing happened to another singer who had a facelift. She was especially concerned about the lines that went from the edge of her nostrils to the corners of her mouth. I told her that as soon as she went back to singing, the lines would come back. She was determined to go ahead and after surgery she lost her voice, or more precisely her audio-vocal control. To begin with, her listening curve became flat—in audiometric terms, amusical. It was all gone: the voice, the pitch control and the quality. After I reeducated her she wound up with a voice that was better than ever—but the lines did come back!

Clearly the larynx is not the specific organ of singing, any more than the strings of a violin are the whole instrument. In singing, the body is the instrument and the vocal cords are the vehicle for making it resonate. If we did not accept the body as the instrument of song and speech, we would be hard pressed to locate an organ of singing.

The primary function of the larynx is to close the glottis upon swallowing. The trachea, through which we breathe, is closed when we swallow by the muscular contraction of the vocal cords and epiglottis. The mobility of the pharynx serves primarily to move food downwards, while ensuring the passage of air for breathing. There is nothing in any of this that predicts the use of the pharynx or larynx in phonation. The nose is essentially a respiratory organ with a rich supply of sympathetic fibers in its mucosa. It acts as a neuro-vegetative antenna. It was originally more important as an olfactory organ, but in man this activity is minimal. In any case, the nose was certainly not made primarily for singing. This is also true of the soft palate, so often spoken of in relation to vocal technique. Its first purpose is to aid in swallowing food by impeding its flow backward into the nasal fossae, just as the epiglottis covers the glottis and for the same reason.

So what do these organs have to do with the voice since their primary function is so far removed from singing? Vocal emission would seem to be a secondary and separate use of the laryngo-pharyngeal-bucal-nasal system. In fact, however, all these organs do work together in phonation. The need for communication is so powerful that it transforms these organs for a use other than the original one, even when those organs are damaged. With human beings, we can count on the extraordinary possibilities of the neuromuscular system. Its adaptive powers are enormous.

Crazy about Singing

Several decades ago, I met someone who was so infatuated with singing that he sang himself silly and quickly damaged his larynx. He came to me on the advice of close friends. His larynx was held tight in his throat and so he pushed. Once the larynx becomes tense, you have to push to produce sound, and the harder you push, the tighter the larynx, until eventually the mechanism unravels and becomes damaged.

Our aspiring singer was destroyed before he ever had a chance to sing professionally. By the time he arrived in my office, he was unable to produce a decent sound. He presented with intracordal nodules, which are very rare. Nodes are normally found at the borders of the cord and indicate that the larynx is making an unnatural effort. With intracordal nodules, the whole cord is infiltrated and nodular. Even worse in his case, both vocal cords bulged identically. That meant they only touched in the center where they bellied out pathologically. As for the voice, all we heard was a rush of air! Still he would not give up hope.

In such circumstances, all you can do is to try to reorganize some sort of functional dynamic. As far as I knew, few cases with such a catastrophic clinical picture could recover. This larynx had been particularly misused. It was clear that his capacity for self-listening must have been minimal and the effect was disastrous. An audiometric examination confirmed that this was so. His situation was even more difficult because he had a Spanish ear, poor in high frequencies by nature. He was from Aragon and spoke with a heavy accent and a completely hoarse voice.

I knew that the cause of his trouble was in his ears. The only advice I could offer was to educate his right ear. His self-confidence was already shaken and my words came as a complete surprise to him. His larynx was suffering and I was talking about his ear! Ridiculous! He smiled politely and went off to get some other opinions.

When he told another specialist that an ENT specialist had told him that the trouble was his ear the response was predictable. "That's crazy!"—The usual response to something new. My colleague determined the problem to be caused by secretions dripping on his cords from perfectly frightful tonsils. My brave Spaniard found his answer; this, at least, was something you could see! The diagnosis sounded so logical that he agreed to have those miserable sponges removed. The operation took place but the tonsils were left largely intact while the soft palate was removed instead in a particularly clumsy surgical procedure. Now, not only was his voice hoarse, but it also had developed a ridiculous nasal quality.

How does one repair a mishap of such dramatic proportions, perhaps by consulting with another specialist? This one twice threw up his hands in horror: first at hearing my diagnosis and then upon observing the effects of a wildly inappropriate and badly executed surgery. Terrible! Especially, explained this knowledgeable doctor, since taking out the tonsils would not have helped. All his misery was caused by a deviated septum that prevented the mucus from draining normally, thereby causing a perpetual postnasal drip. Nothing for it but more surgery! The septum was removed all too effectively. Not only the cartilage and the medial bone but also the nasal pyramid and the mucous membrane were removed. The result was an enormous hole between the nasal faucae. He had the nose of a washed-up prizefighter.

Everything had gone from bad to worse. It took great courage, I suspect, for our young fellow to seek yet another opinion. The last surgeon took whatever was left, namely, the turbinate bones of the nasal fossae. What in hell could have possessed this specialist? He further enlarged the hole of the nasal fossae, unleashing a cataclysmic hemorrhage! Months had passed. It takes time to create that kind of mess, and our brave Spaniard, virtually "ENT-ed" to death was still not singing. He was in terrible shape.

My friends who had recommended me to him knew every detail of the unhappy pilgrimage of their protégé. They asked me if I would see their pet once more. And so, there was my "nodular larynx" again, just as damaged as ever. He had shreds of tonsils, and in place of a soft palate he had only a rigid strip of tissue, too short and too tight with scar tissue. His nose had a room inside as big as a cathedral, and was loaded with crusts. Nature abhors a vacuum and it tried to compensate with abundant secretions. But the mucous membrane was already totally lacking in tone, indicating that it was dying.

What next? Certainly no more operations. Later on, perhaps reconstructive surgery to restore the nasal pyramid and to give him a decent profile. For the time being, I gave him some practical advice on how to balance the airflow in the nasal fossae. Singing was obviously out of question. He could only get worse, not better. His phonation was so altered that he had great difficulty speaking. To help him with this, I could only repeat my offer of auditory reeducation. Although the chances of success had been greatly diminished, I had such a faith in auditory rehabilitation that I started treatment full of enthusiasm.

As the auditory reeducation of the singer was beginning, I was visited by a group of professionals from the University of Marseilles who came to learn more about my activities. The chairman of the ENT department examined our veteran of multiple bad surgeries. All that remained intact were the intracordal nodules. Faced with this unforgettable clinical picture, the ENT specialist whispered surreptitiously, "I wouldn't give two centimes for your chances to rehabilitate this guy!"

Three or four weeks later, at his invitation, I went to Marseilles to give a conference on new developments in phono-audiology. I brought along my patient who, though still in rehabilitation, had recovered his speaking voice and was able to sing. He was living testimony of the power of the reeducation of the ear, without any other treatment.

The therapy that continued for another two months made a professional singing career possible for him. He was engaged at the theater of Chatelet as a leading tenor. He often stood in for Luis Mariano. As he approached his fiftieth birthday, he left his career to live in Spain with his family and all his old friends. There he began to teach the method of vocal reeducation that had helped him.

This adventure sounds like a fairy tale even now as I write about it. I marvel at the conclusive proof that it offers.

Prompted by listening, the ear takes over the body and organizes all the connections necessary for communication. Humanity's intense desire to live in community has produced singing and speaking. The internal organization that acts on phonation depends solely on the induction brought about by listening. From this case, we can see that even a severely impaired larynx can recover its function when deficient listening is treated and restored. Damaged organs can recover their full capacity. What is more, the synergetic action of these organs will result in a new adaptation of the structure of phonation despite surgical damage or disease. Most exciting and important is that the desire to listen has enormous power to induce change.

CHAPTER 6

THE ART OF SINGING

Numerous requirements must be met to attain a professional level of singing. The voice is certainly a determining factor but you also need a solidly-based vocation, and you must sing with absolute mastery. Furthermore, you must be an excellent musician and interpreter, qualities rarely found in the same individual. Without them, even an exceptionally beautiful voice is not sufficient. The goal is a vibrant body that consistently produces high quality sounds, in both singing and speaking. Consummate mastery is necessary to attain this level. Control in singing is achieved through the integration of knowledge, mental attitude, and good alignment. As a result, energy increases, alertness sharpens, more intense concentration becomes possible, and excellent vocal emission can be acquired, but to acquire it requires a special aptitude. It is true that some singers fill halls and resonate with a vast public without having any technique. But their careers make no mark on the history of singing. To be numbered among the great requires singing smarts, sensitivity, imagination, and intelligence.

I remember a tenor at the *Capitole* in Toulouse who let out a gargantuan crack on a high C in *William Tell*. He was not the least disturbed by the catcalls erupting from the gallery. In order to redeem himself, he sang the aria over again, this time with a well-sung high C. It changed the opinion of the audience. Still not content, he sang the same aria all over again first a half tone higher and then again a whole tone higher, making that a high "D" just to prove that he could do it. This kind of behavior would be unacceptable today, even in Toulouse, where the appreciation of singing as an athletic event is still extreme. (We assume that this was during a recital with piano accompaniment as it is unlikely that the orchestra would have parts available in three different keys.)

As a child, I often heard a member of the audience at the *Capitole* sing out a note or even a whole phrase that the singer on the stage had just blown. Such antics are more suited to stadiums. Where is the intelligence in treating a high note like a home run? In the past many opera lovers would show up to hear a single note or a bravura passage, the same way that cycling fans wake up only for the sprint.

It seems amazing that even the *Capitole* in Toulouse could be the scene of a show like the one I once attended. In *La Favorite*, there was an immense prima donna with a beautiful voice. The tenor, from Toulouse, was singing his umpteenth farewell performance. He still had some good notes, but he was a little guy and a lousy actor. Doubtless compensating for the mismatch of his small stature and his huge tenor voice, he tried to fill the stage by running all over the place, waving his arms in all directions.

During the duet, he charged his partner and grabbed her as well as he could around the lower trunk! As he embraced this monolith, she stood absolutely still. Then he abandoned his amorous statue to finish her duet alone while he marched right down to the footlights and turned the performance into a shouting match. Today such a scene would make a delightful comedy sketch. At the time, it inspired admiration in a certain sort of opera fan. Many works such as *La Juive*, *Les Huguenots*, and *Robert le Diable* belong to the heyday of the clarion voice. Then it was okay for an artist to save himself all night and come to life only in a signature passage.

Movies and television have created a taste for dramatic acting that has extended to opera. In the last decades, opera has undergone a metamorphosis, sometimes to excess. This new passion can lead people to ignore vocalism. Good sound depends on a certain static quality, including facial expressions too bland to express the meaning of the words.

The beginner will study singing with more enthusiasm if he understands the process. Once he feels the need to sing, he will want to know more about it. There are so many different ways to begin singing! I refer not only to different schools of singing that claim to have primacy over others, but also to choice of expression: an aria or song, a show tune or something more intimate. Some will be closer to speech, others will be built on vocalization, or combine any musical characteristics the human spirit can invent. Then, there is sacred song, calling upon its own set of psychological and mental attitudes.

There are songs for the body and songs for the spirit. It is true that we cannot completely separate the two, but it is also true that they exist on different levels. The body is a dynamic entity that expresses itself through gesture and language. Where gesture is manifest, the form of expression moves closer to dance. Body and spirit overlap, in each case with its own emphasis, but the difference is not purely conceptual. In a military song, for example, the words follow a musical cadence designed to sustain marching. In functional terms, the vestibule is stimulated by rhythmic cadences that invite the entire body to march. With the dance as well, the vestibule directs the body according to the sounds it perceives. Sounds and songs make the body move by conditioning an irresistible neuro-muscular response. The body resonates and movement gains ascendancy over thought. The person subjected to these acoustic phenomena seems possessed by them.

We cannot assign the same meaning to all singing, because there are various modes of expression. Yet a certain communality exists in opera and orchestral repertoire, songs for recital, popular songs, and sacred singing, although each type of singing will need to adapt the technique somewhat to its own purposes. In lyric singing or in song, even in popular song, the text is the support on which the music is constructed and harmonized. In a lied, for example, there is a fit between the poetry, which already sings on its own, and the musical expression, which reinforces the text. This combination gives the text a particular feeling created by the composer. Through study and reflection, the singer can assume the psychological attitude of the composer and may even take on the same physical feelings as well. This special state allows the singer to manifest the resonance that the musician created in the poetic text.

Singing begins with mastering a technique until it becomes automatic, then immersing oneself in the text and evoking the musical form. This kind of interpretation adds dimension to the text. When this work is accomplished there is a fit, signifying that text and music are profoundly conveyed. Whatever the mode of expression, great singing technique remains constant. The process is identical for generating sound in the larynx, especially with regard to bone transmission and with respect to vowels, just as a good instrumentalist uses the same technique for every type of music. So even if an aria from *Tosca* and a piece of Gregorian Chant sound completely different, it is only the use of technique that changes.

What, then, are the characteristics of each type of singing? They are easy to detect if we bear in mind that singing has several consequences. When the singer transmits his proprioceptive sensations to the listener, along with words and music, he plays upon the body of the listener. A good singer does this with ease because the audience receives him gladly. These perceptual transfers, together with interpretation and vocal quality, are fundamental to the appreciation of good singing.

So if aria and chant are produced in exactly the same way, they are perceived so differently because they transmit totally opposite proprioceptive sensations. The opera singer's purpose is to transport the listener to emotional heights that are global, physically active, and visceral. Songs of incantation that erase the awareness of the body and its characteristic proprioceptive sensations induce a different state, that of trance. In Gregorian chant, the monk aims to reduce emotional reactivity as much as possible. No tempo is imposed but there is a deliberate internal search. Deeper and more rhythmic breathing induces the cardiac muscle to acquire the slow, peaceful, fundamental systole-diastole cadence on which the modulations of Gregorian chant are based. It is not, in and of itself, sacred, but its mode of production can transport us to a consciousness specific to the sacred. To reach this state, it is necessary to have gathered a tremendous amount of energy, as when we prepare to meditate or pray. To stay on this level requires absolute quiet in the body.

Opera and chant are different because the attitude of the vocalist differs. Keep in mind the energy charge that arises from singing. Opera provides a substantial amount of stimulation, with emotional participation so intense that it simultaneously discharges an important amount of energy. Gregorian chant invokes minimal involvement of the body as we are accustomed to hear it and minimal discharge of energy. All sacred singing is designed to optimally increase our dynamic recharge.

PART II

HOW THE EAR WORKS

CHAPTER 7

ABOUT LISTENING

We now turn to the theoretical aspects of singing with information useful for beginners, professional singers, and teachers. Teachers will find techniques for reaching students that might otherwise be unteachable: people with unattractive voices or those who sing out of tune. They will learn how to bring students along quickly, shortening or eliminating plateaus.

The Perceptual Basis of Listening

Listening is a very high-level perceptual function. To hear is to identify a sound passively as when we hear someone talking to us without paying attention to what they are saying.

As soon as we decide to listen to a speaker's every word, or to every musical note, we engage—we mobilize our whole body—and shift our nervous system to an active body-mind dynamic. Active listening regulates the entire cybernetics of vocal emission.

Whoever emits a sound, whether sung or spoken, is the first to hear the sound produced, when he perceives it mentally, but whether or not he is listening to himself and others is another matter. The rewards of listening to our inner voice without the masking effects of language are immediate. We all have a kind of knowing that comes to us from our inner voice. We may think of it as intuition, or call it a hunch or a feeling in the bones. In fact, it is bone conduction that brings this voice to us. When you pay attention to it, life becomes suddenly simpler. You can break free from the bonds of emotional dependency by attending to the wisdom you carry within. When you decide to listen, you will easily adopt a healthy attitude, for it is the will that motivates action. Personal growth always involves a deepening of our ability to listen.

What is the Nature of Listening?

We have only begun to understand the ear, the organ of singing. Without it no language can exist. Hearing takes place along a continuum that goes from deafness to the acquisition of the ideal ear. It comprises countless ways of hearing and listening that influence the way we speak and even more with the way we sing. The ear must be understood in relationship to all the organs involved in singing: the larynx, the lungs, and that part of the mouth and pharynx activated by phonation. We will also touch on the interaction between the ear and the nervous system to clarify the body's role in phonation.

The chapters that follow explore the role of the ear, starting with the simplest notions and moving towards the more complex, each accompanied by diagrams. The technical language can be quite complex but once you have mastered it you can use it when you talk to about vocal technique. Start with the parts that most interest you. Eventually it will all start to make sense. Then you can go back to pick up the parts you skipped. We begin the anatomo-physioneurology of the ear, with the main mechanisms that regulate the functioning of its three auditory structures. We will consider the way the nervous system works with the ear to execute commands at the cortical level and the control responses of the organs of phonation as well as those that occur throughout the body.

CHAPTER 8

ANATOMY AND PHYSIOLOGY

The anatomy and physiology of the ear is very complex. What follows is a simplified overview. Some aspects of the ear's internal functioning are still being debated. In this discussion I will present only established facts. This way, we will stay on firm ground. We only need to know what goes into the ear and what comes out as vocal emission. The rest is the province of specialists—and they disagree on many points.

The ear has tremendous influence over the nervous system given that;

1. The ear is the first sensory organ to become operational. It appears in the first days after conception. It grows with a rapidity that surpasses understanding, and is complete and functional by the fourth month of pregnancy. By the fifth month of gestation, the inner ear is a fully-grown organ, ready to store information.
2. The ear controls an important neuronal network that is also astonishing in its precocity. The oldest part of the ear, the vestibular labyrinth, makes its way into the neural tube, which, from the fifth month of pregnancy, becomes the operating nervous system. The subsequent motor system is born already under its control. The other part of the ear, the cochlea, which is more focused on listening, reaches out simultaneously to most parts of the encephalon (brain) in order to record sounds.
3. No other organ of the human body, it seems to me, shows such precocity and thus prevails so completely. It is this particular evolution that destines man to become a listener. The ear rapidly builds a structure with several levels, making up the "first brain," which I call the "vestibular brain." Later on, it is joined by the "cochlear brain."

(By some time around the fifth month of gestation, the inner ear is complete and can process sound. However, other parts of the ear, the integration with the nervous system, and the developing brain continue until at least the second year of life. Initially the ear perceives only low frequencies, because individual hair cells change responsiveness during development. Cells at the base of the cochlea mature first and initially respond to low tones, but as the properties of the basilar membrane change, the hair cells become sensitive to progressively higher frequencies, while newly maturing hair cells, closer to the apex of the cochlea, take over low frequency reception. Consult the bibliography for further, up to date, information.)

Anatomy

The Inner Ear

The inner ear is located deep in the side of the skull. It is contained in a non-compact bone shaped like a pyramid with the apex oriented forward and inward. The inner ear looks like a bony pocket and is called the labyrinthine vesicle or bony labyrinth (see fig. 8.1). The structure of its shell is dense. It contains the membranous labyrinth made up of the vestibule and the cochlea. Because of the various elements contained in its structure, the membranous labyrinth has a complex appearance. Though well defined, it is difficult, if not impossible, to distinguish the common ties joining the various parts of these elements within the inner ear.

The membranous labyrinth is a unique functional entity whose activities are characterized by an increasing power of detection that makes it possible to analyze body movements and to decipher and analyze minute sound waves as they move through the air. We shall see this when we look closely at the dynamic of the inner ear.

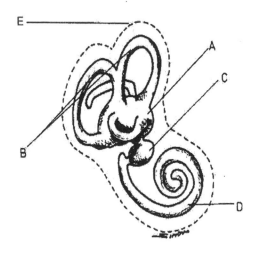

Figure 8.1 Inner Ear

A
B } vestibule
C
D   cochlear
E   bony labyrinth

} membranous labyrinth

The membranous labyrinth is made up of two organs: one called the vestibule, the other one called the cochlea.

The vestibule is made up of the saccule, and the utricle, topped by the semicircular canals (see fig. 8.2). It is the oldest part of the ear and consists of the utricle, which organizes movements, predominantly on the horizontal plane, especially at the level of the head; the saccule, which organizes movements primarily on the vertical plane, especially at the level of the spinal column; and semicircular canals, which are nearly at right angles to one another. This arrangement allows the detection of movement in all directions and makes it possible for the body to move in the three axes of space.

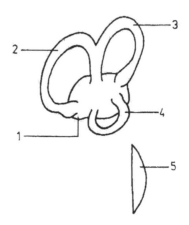

Figure 8.2 Schematic of the Vestibule

1. Utricle. 2. Posterior semicircular canal. 3. Superior semicircular canal. 4. Lateral or horizontal semicircular canal. 5. Saccule.

The cochlea is so named because it looks like a snail shell and forms two and a half spirals from bottom to top. It appears after the vestibule in phylogenic development as well as in the ontogenetic domain and is dedicated to audition (hearing).

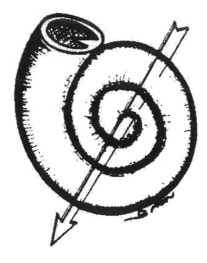

Figure 8.3 The Cochlea

The Middle Ear

The middle ear (see fig. 8.4) is located between the external and inner ear. It is composed of three ossicles which, starting with the innermost, are named as follows:

- the stirrup or stapes,
- the anvil or incus, and
- the hammer or malleus.

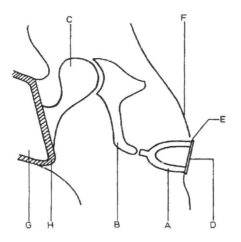

Figure 8.4 Middle Ear

A. Stirrup. B. Incus or anvil. C. Hammer. D. Oval window. E. Oval window. F. Inner ear. G. External auditory conduit. H. Eardrum.

A footplate attaches the stirrup to the oval window, one of two windows opening into the wall of the cochlea. The oval window is sealed by a flexible membrane. The tip of the stirrup joins the lower and interior tip of the anvil, the median ossicle, which is rigidly attached to the hammer. The hammer is the third of the ossicles and the most external one. It is linked to the tympanic membrane or eardrum by its handle. The tympanic membrane is the dividing structure between the external ear and the middle ear and it seals the opening on the side of the external ear.

The middle ear connects with the mastoid in the rear and with the eustachian tube in the front, thus joining the ear with the pharynx. As the diagram shown in the highly schematic figure 8.5 illustrates, the eustachian tube, as seen from above, is oblique in its course toward the front and middle of the body. The diagram also shows the external auditory canal as well as part of the inner ear which contains the labyrinth.

There are two muscles in the middle ear and both are of paramount importance (see fig. 8.6). They are largely responsible for regulating the ear and are thus the controls for the listening function. These muscles, the muscle of the stirrup and the muscle of the hammer, will feature prominently throughout the rest of this book.

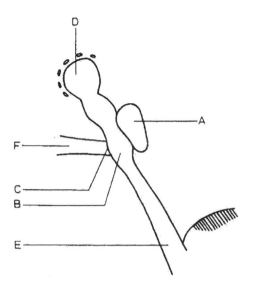

Figure 8.5 Middle Ear

A. Inner ear. B. Shell of tympanum. C. Tympanic
membrane. D. Mastoid. E. Eustachian tube. F. External
auditory conduit.

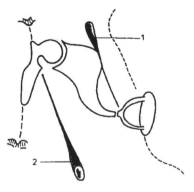

Figure 8.6 Muscles of the Middle Ear

1. Muscle of the stirrup. 2. Muscle of the hammer.

The External Ear

This is the visible part of the ear. It includes the auricle and the external auditory canal, which is sealed by the tympanic membrane.

Physiology

Following this short summary of anatomy, elements that contribute to at least a partial understanding of how the ear functions will be presented. As with the anatomy, the description proceeds from the inside out, beginning with the inner ear, moving to the middle ear and finishing with the external ear.

The Inner Ear

The membranous labyrinth contains hair cells, which are receptors. They are located in different places to respond to different functions:

- On the floor of the utricle,
- In the ampullae of the semicircular canals,
- On the perpendicular face of the saccule, and finally,
- In the basilar membrane of the organ of Corti, which analyzes frequencies.

The function of the inner ear is to analyze movements, rhythms, and sequences of frequencies or pitch. The various parts of the ear have different shapes to help them carry out their different tasks (see fig. 8.7). The inner ear is the organ of listening, calling for a specific posture, a dynamic interaction with the environment, and very focused attention.

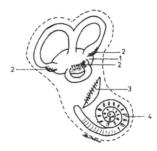

Figure 8.7 Inner Ear

1. Utricle. 2. Ampullae of the semicircular canal.
3. Saccule. 4. Cochlea.

The vestibule measures movement of great amplitude, namely the movement of the body. The cochlea measures infinitesimal movements, those of sounds. It is designed to work with the vestibule, and is made of the same material, but is organized differently to assume complementary functions. The adaptive mechanisms of the inner ear are complex, allowing it to analyze the extremely subtle movements caused by acoustic impulses on a molecular level as well as gross body movement, occurring on a scale of far greater magnitude.

The inner ear is a single entity. Any dysfunction of one of its parts leads to a more or less marked dysfunction of the entire system. Optimal efficiency of the cochlea, for instance, requires good positioning of the vestibule. As we study more listening and singing, we will learn how the vestibule is positioned. This is most important, since the vestibule controls all the muscles of the body, those necessary to maintain upright stature but also, in a more subtle way, the muscles involved in posture. When the posture is correct, the vestibule is well positioned and, consequently, the cochlea can work optimally. The result is good hearing, excellent listening, and perfect body control, all elements promoting good control of the voice.

The Middle Ear

Excellent listening is most likely when accompanied by exceedingly functional hearing. Fitness of muscles in the middle ear makes possible the optimal use of the inner ear. This requires an ongoing coordination between the muscles of the hammer and the stirrup. Under optimal conditions, these muscles act synergistically rather than antagonistically. Their reciprocal actions induce an optimal tone resulting from a balance between the flexor muscles and the extensor muscles.

The muscle of the stirrup is an extensor; the muscle of the hammer is a flexor. The muscle of the stirrup regulates the inner ear. It is the last of the extensors to have developed and controls a set of synergies that will be described in the chapter about posture.

The regulatory system controlled by the ear impacts the whole body and prepares it for singing. In fact, to "prick one's ears" is to open them. Moreover, it also opens the entire body by acting on all the extensors.

The physiology of the auditory system allows for the possibility of harmonious interplay between the muscles of the hammer and the stirrup. It balances the tensions between both muscles, reaching a point of equilibrium. When one muscle dominates, it can be seen immediately in the listening test. If the two muscles act in concert, and each has the same divided tension, the test shows an "ideal profile."

A dislocated curve is observed as soon as one of the muscles prevails. For example, a functional disharmony appears when the muscle of the stirrup, the extensor, takes over. The regulation in the internal chamber of the inner ear is no longer optimal, resulting in too great an absorption of the endolymph fluid and causing a muting of the high frequencies. Thus, high frequencies are not perceived and the hammer-stirrup block moves backward and outward, further decreasing acute perception of high frequencies while increasing the receipt of low frequencies.

The action of the extensor becomes greatly exaggerated in this case. This hyperextension spreads throughout the body, impacting all of the extensor muscles, precluding good vocal emission. There is also disharmony in the interplay of the antagonistic flexor-extensor pairs because of the exaggerated tension of the extensor muscles. The posture is therefore somewhat overcorrected. This looks as though there is a sort of hyper-opening in the general posture which, in the extreme, seems to override the role of the flexors. The result is a stiff "military" posture.

The opposite can also be true. Excessive tension in the muscle of the hammer also precludes an excellent posture for singing. This type of perceptual disturbance reduces auditory control necessary for singing by eliminating too many low frequencies. A series of simultaneous signs manifests as difficulty in integrating one's body image. In psychological jargon, it means that the person is cut off from the perception of his body as an instrument. He is like a musician who no longer knows his instrument. He will seem under-energized and clumsy.

The right muscular balance is important. This is true for the ear as well as for the whole body. Each one reveals the other. Having understood this, one becomes aware that singing requires the naturally existing tensions between the flexor muscles and the tensor muscles to balance each other. Any breach of balance appreciably modifies vocal emission, in a way that is apparent to the well-trained ear.

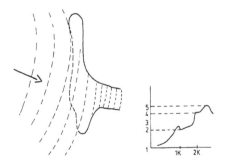

Figure 8.8

The Influence of the External Auditory Conduit on the Sound Wave.

The External Ear

The external ear developed last on both the phylogenetic and ontogenetic levels. It is both an amplifier and a filter, (see fig.8.8) favoring the diffusion of certain sounds into the inner ear, especially high frequencies

The different physiological schemata presented in this chapter serve to explain the connection between the ear and the nervous system. The neurology of the ear in the next chapter is simplified and contains only information relevant to the role of the ear in singing.

CHAPTER 9

THE EAR AND THE NERVOUS SYSTEM

When we speak, the whole body participates, and in singing, the participation of the body along with the nervous system is even greater. For this reason, it is important to understand the connections between the inner ear and the nervous system, particularly those between the ear and the brain. Starting from the inside we will study the inner ear and its vast network of neurons, then the nervous system as it relates to the middle ear, and finally the external ear will be explored.

The Inner Ear

The inner ear is regulated by two large networks that I call integrators. I will describe only the main pathways that make it possible to understand the connections between the ear and the body in singing. The two integrators are the vestibular integrator and the cochlear integrator. Although I will focus on each one separately, remember that there are many connections between those two systems and they function as a single entity.

The Vestibular Integrator

The vestibular integrator is related to the vestibule, which is made up of the utricle topped by semicircular canals and the saccule. I also call it the somatic integrator since it automatically controls the motor and sensory responses of the entire body. The functions of the vestibular integrator usually operate outside of our conscious control. All sensory and motor learning must first be integrated through willful and conscious efforts, starting with sitting, then standing and walking, etc. When all the sequential steps fall correctly into place, our attention is freed so that we can focus on further development. There is a specific process that leads from a conscious, purposeful vigilance to the development of an automatic dynamic which is free of constraint.

But let's go back to the vestibular integrator (see fig. 9.1). The utricular, ampular, and saccular nerves are the components of the vestibular nerve, which emerges from the vestibule and meets in Scarpa's ganglion. The nerve is then directed toward four nuclei and thence to the ventral (front of the body) roots of the spinal column. These motor roots became a two-way street, while they are exercising their control over the whole of the body's musculature; they are themselves cybernetically dependent on vestibular control. These nerve fibers are the homolateral vestibulo-spinal tracts (or spinal tracts of Deiter) and the contralateral vestibulo-spinal tracts, emerging from Roller's nucleus. All of these systems come under the control of the vestibule.

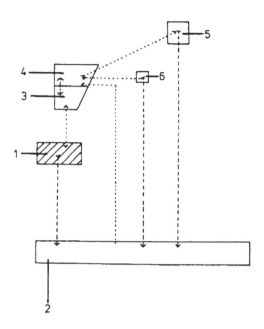

Figure 9.1 Vestibular Integrator

1. Vestibule. 2. Body. 3. Cerebellum. 4. Paleo-Cerebellum.
5. Red nucleus. 6. Bulbar olive.

Any act of motor control results in a counterreaction. This takes place through nerve fascicles that are collected in the cerebellum, which is an important annex of the vestibule. The internal, most archaic part of the cerebellum, the archeo-cerebellum, captures the projection of the vestibule itself while the adjunct part, the paleo-cerebellum, perceives the projection of the entire body.

Because of a particularly active network of cells on the surface of the cerebellum, many connections link each point of the vestibule with a point on the body. Consequently, there is direct interaction between the vestibule and the body. Additional pathways from the paleo-cerebellum to the red nucleus and the olivary nucleus lock in the system's connections. The main point to remember in this intentionally brief description is that the ear is a single unit. Whether static or dynamic, the whole motor body is under the strict control of the vestibule. As we shall see again in later chapters of this book, this is a fact of major importance when it comes to singing.

The Cochlear Integrator

The second part of the inner ear, the cochlea, plays a different role, although it is also linked to the vestibule in various ways. It provides the encephalon with all its higher functions: audition and thus listening, language and the automatic cerebral motor perceptions. These occupy the greater part of the cortex, while leaving considerable space to the optic nerve.

The following schema, (fig. 9.2) illustrates the cochlear integrator, also called the linguistic integrator.

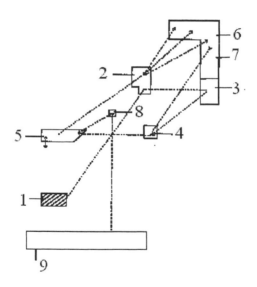

Figure 9.2 Cochlear Integrator

1. Cochlea. 2. Thalamus. 3. Temporal cortex. 4. Pons.
5. Cerebellum. 6. Frontal lobe. 7. Parietal lobe.
8. Thalamus. 9. Cortex.

This circuit touches the cochlea, the thalamus, the cortex, the pons, the cerebellum, the thalamus, and then back to the cortex in succession before extending to new areas. There is an important infusion of information into the red nucleus directed to the anterior roots of the medulla, constituting another circuit connected to the vestibular fasciculus. Furthermore, the cortical area is "projected" on the neo-cerebellum, a more recent and the most external part of the brain.

This cortical area, by virtue of the superficial network, is the projective system of the vestibular nerve. It makes it possible to install analogous differential responses connected to the anterior areas of the paleo-cerebellum and the archeo-cerebellum.

A more comprehensive description would also include: the visual integrator, the pyramidal integrator which I call "the driver."

Figure 9.3 illustrates the ear-brain system with particular emphasis on the visual integrator. The diagram shows the complexity and highly integrated nature of the interrelationships between the ear and the brain. The feedback loops permit extensive control.

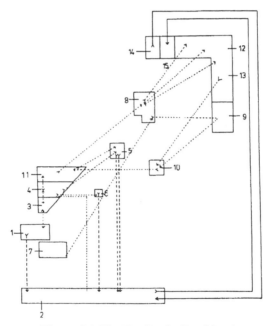

Figure 9.3 The Ear-Brain Combination

Vestibular integrator: 1. Vestibule. 2. Body. 3. Forebrain. 4. Paleo-cerebellum. 5. Red nucleus (thalamus). 6. Olive nucleus.
Cochlear Integrator: 7. Cochlea. 8. Thalamus.
9. Temporal lobe. 10. Pons. 11. Neo-cerebellum.
12. Frontal cortex. 13 Parietal lobe.
The Conductor: 14. Pyramidal fasciculus. 15. Sensory return fasciculus.

The Middle Ear

Neurologically speaking, two systems are at work in the middle ear:

- The first is under the control of the facial nerve which innervates the muscle of the stirrup,
- The second system is under the control of the trigeminal nerve, or fifth cranial nerve, which innervates the muscle of the hammer.

This is extremely important when we use a neurological approach to understanding how the ear functions; we realize that the human ear is divided in two parts and not three as is usually thought. The first part includes the inner ear, which is regulated by the muscle of the stirrup. This muscle is located in the middle ear and is innervated by the facial nerve, which simultaneously controls all the muscles of the face and the platysma in the neck. The second part includes the external ear, in particular the tympanic membrane or eardrum which is regulated by the muscle of the hammer. This muscle is innervated by the trigeminal nerve, which also controls the muscles of mastication.

So, on the one hand, the stirrup and its muscle maintain a stable pressure of the liquids within the inner ear. On the other hand, the hammer and the anvil regulate the tympanic pressure in response to the sounds that one wishes to perceive. In addition, different control systems come into play to protect the ear as soon as the intensity of the volume crosses a certain threshold. Finally, let's not forget that the Eustachian tube assumes a role in the mechanisms which regulate the middle ear.

Figure 9.4 shows some of these mechanisms at work. Neurological connections exist between the two parts of the ear just described and some organs of phonation. They all have the same embryological origin and act in synergy when we speak or sing. For instance, the lower jaw is derived from a cartilaginous plate called Meckel's cartilage, which developed out of the embryonic first branchial arch. A part of this cartilage also forms the basis of two of the ossicles of the middle ear: the anvil and the hammer. The link between the ear and some parts of the face involved in speech begin developing at conception.

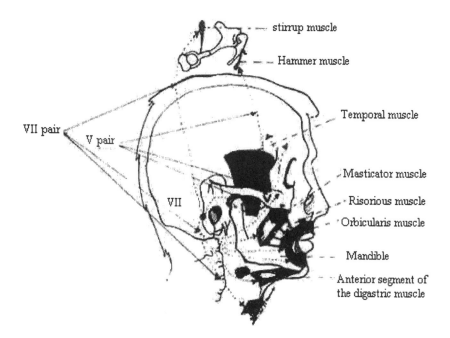

Figure 9.4

The side view face shows the lower mandible, the muscles of mastication (masseter and temporalis) and their antagonist (the anterior belly of the digastric
muscle). In addition, you can see the innervation of the muscles of mastication
by the trigeminal nerve (fifth cranial nerve pair) and the innervation of all the
muscles of the face by the facial nerve (seventh cranial nerve pair). Finally, for
a better understanding, the middle ear, the three ossicles, the muscle of the
hammer, and the muscle of the stirrup are shown above the profile. This presentation makes it easier to visualize the nerve pathways, one coming from the
trigeminal nerve towards the muscle of the hammer, the other coming from the
facial nerve toward the muscle of the stirrup.

Note that the musculature of the mandible and that of the hammer are controlled by the same nerve: the lower maxillary nerve, a branch of the trigeminal
or fifth cranial nerve. That means there is a constant relationship between the
tension of the tympanic membrane, regulated by the muscle of the hammer, and
the mobility of the lower jaw adjusting the motions of the mandible, and therefore of the mouth as one sings. If there is trouble with coordination [200Hz]
there will be difficulty with articulation, and the facial muscles will contract into
strange grimaces. You can no doubt think of at least one singer currently on the
scene who makes faces while singing.

Other parts of the ear connected with singing or speaking evolve from the second brachial arch of the embryo. The stirrup, which soon becomes equipped with its muscle (a fact of considerable importance in the mechanics of hearing), originates from the second brachial arch. Also emanating from this branch are:

- The upper part of the larynx,
- The hyoid bone to which some muscles of the tongue are attached,
- The ligaments and muscles that fasten the hyoid bone to the stylohyoid process,
- The anterior belly of the digastric muscle which is an antagonist to the mucles of mastication, and
- The muscles of the face.

As with the first brachial arch, the muscle of the stirrup and the muscles of the face near the seventh cranial nerve, also known as the facial nerve, share a common innervation. Here again, we observe a continuous link between the ear and the mechanisms of phonation.

The External Ear

From a neurological point of view, we observe that several branches of the fifth and seventh cranial nerves maintain the sensitivity of both the external ear and the auditory canal. The eardrum, which belongs to both the external and middle ear since it separates them, is innervated by several cranial nerves, including a major nerve that plays a crucial role in singing. This is the pneumogastric nerve, also called the vagus.

The Vagus Nerve

The vagus nerve plays an essential role in the act of singing as well as in speaking. It has several tasks. Usually, nerves are either motor with direct command over muscles, or sensory if their task is to refer perceptual information. Some are both somatic motor and sensory. For instance, the fifth cranial nerve gives the face its sensitivity but also allows the mobility of the jaws.

The vagus nerve combines all of these functions. It is somatic, motor, sensory, and parasympathetic, giving it the ability to regulate the abdominal viscera. Moreover, it spreads over an immense area of the human body. Its contribution to phonation is fundamental. It is by design asymmetrical, with the right branch being shorter than the left. It emanates from the base of the skull, sends several sensory fibers to the dura mater covering of the brain, and then divides into various branches.

Let's begin with a closer look at the right vagus nerve. It is most important to remember that one of its branches innervates both the lower part of the external auditory canal and the tympanic membrane. This is its only external point of emergence but it plays an enormous role. It is also important to emphasize that the vagus nerve extends a sensory nerve fiber onto the muscle of the stirrup, which receives its motor activation from the facial nerve.

The vagus nerve, working in association with the glossopharyngeal nerve, innervates the eustachian tube and the pharynx. It also supplies sensory innervation to the larynx through the upper laryngeal nerve and provides motor function to the larynx through the lower laryngeal nerve, also called the recurrent nerve. This name is derived from the loop that this nerve makes around the right subclavian artery.

The right vagus nerve then innervates the bronchi, the esophagus, and the coronary arteries. From there it descends through the diaphragm near the pylorus, generously innervates the lesser curvature of the stomach, and fuses with the left vagus nerve behind it.

The left vagus nerve is identical to the right one, except for its greater length. Notice that this branch of the recurrent nerve reaches the larynx by looping back around the aorta. The left vagus nerve then runs across the abdomen and reaches most of the visceral organs, the small intestine, colon, and sigmoid colon, ending at the level of the anal sphincter. As it descends, it carries fibers to the spleen, the pancreas, the kidneys, the suprarenal glands, etc. It ends in the gall bladder after having provided the pelvic plexus and the sacral plexus with associated nerve fibers via connections called anastomoses.

The vagus nerve exerts an important influence on the parasympathetic system because stimulating the external branch of the vagus nerve, which innervates the tympanic membrane, will also stimulate the following:

- The pharynx,
- The sensory larynx,
- The motor larynx,
- The bronchi,
- The coronary arteries,
- The stomach,
- All the viscera, and finally
- The gall bladder.

This nerve covers an immense area and forms the greatest part of the parasympathetic system. It balances with the sympathetic nervous system, which, like the parasympathetic system, is part of the autonomic nervous system.

The main function of the sympathetic nervous system is to maintain equilibrium in the vital rhythms of the body: cardiac, respiratory, nutritional, or reproductive. It should echo the fundamental, cosmic rhythms that control our most instinctual and essential behaviors. This is not always the case: our behavior may disturb these vital rhythms through the action of the parasympathetic system. The parasympathetic system is often burdened by too much information and blocks the optimal state of balance which should exist between both sympathetic and parasympathetic systems under ideal circumstances. The impact of this imbalance is demonstrated by respiratory insufficiency or by the alteration of the cardiac rhythm and other body rhythms.

A great many psychosomatic symptoms result from disharmony between these two fundamental and complementary systems. Even without going into more detail, it is easy to understand the impact of the vagus nerve on singing. It is this nerve that helps the singer to consciously rediscover the correct respiratory rhythm as well as the cardiac and visceral rhythms so that a synergy is created between this internal network and the larynx, the posture, the attitude, and so forth.

The role of the vagus nerve in singing is clear. It is equally important in mastering a fluid and correct verbal flow in speech. The same synergy must take place if we are to have a coherent and orderly train of thought. Without doubt, singing well is one of the best ways to free ourselves from the burden of parasympathetic or neuropsychological imbalances. I do not know better therapy than the one induced by the voice. But for this therapy to work, further liberation must take place first: that of knowing how to listen.

CHAPTER 10

THE EAR'S CONTROL OF THE VOICE

We will now look at the mechanisms that regulate singing as it is controlled by the ear. Everything, from the smallest cell in the body to the entire cosmos, is subject to rules of control. Cybernetics is the science of the mechanisms of control. Although this claims to be a new science, it is based on principles as old as time. Plato touched on these laws in his writings about government. They are as impossible to transgress as they are timeless.

In cybernetic terms, a system is regulated when its functioning is subject to a control. Each organ of the human body controls a specific function. Only a few aberrations in our behavior are, at times, not cybernetically well mastered. As we move towards effective listening uncontrolled behavior occurs less often.

There is nothing complicated about singing. Every sound that a singer makes follows rules that are controlled by the listening function. The whole art is to abandon yourself, to allow all the regulatory processes, or cybernetic loops, to operate by themselves. A cybernetic loop is a circuit that has a circular path, with the end returning to the beginning. The act of singing is controlled by a number of such circuits. They need to be identified, coordinated, and freed from defects caused by bad usage. Once returned to their original, automatic function, these circuits can operate free of constraint, creating varied and infinite possibilities for the voice, and the voice is then protected from injury.

The organ of control for singing is the ear and the whole system is under the control of the listening function. Figure 10.1 shows an intention to sing which reaches the brain and then brings about the act of singing.

As soon as you make a sound, auditory control is set in motion, collecting a part of the sounds produced in order to maintain control. This sampling of information is sent to the brain so that singing proceeds according to the original intent. In short, a feedback loop is set up. The sequence is as follows: I want to sing. I sing. My ear tells me that I am singing exactly what I wanted to sing. I continue to sing and to monitor myself. This creates a continuous feedback loop. Auditory control is active and equipped with the ability to select what the singer wants to hear when he mentally previews what he will sing and knows how to respond to what the brain plans. Auditory control knows what it needs to master; it makes constant adjustments to insure that the results match the intention. But the ear also regulates the emission and aligns it with what the brain wants to receive.

The ear exercises continuous auditory control. It knows what it is going to hear, so the control is preprogrammed, and assumes the listening posture in order to perceive what it must apprehend. The central nervous system receives the command and refers what it has received.

Yet, the ear acts in concert with the nervous system, which also makes demands on auditory controls, adding afferent motor impulses to direct the motor apparatus. Each part of the body that is activated responds on a centralized level so that sensory-motor control conforms to the ear's demands.

Everything about singing is organized around the ear; it is the superior regulator. The buck stops there. How does this come about? The ear has a double role, based on two polarities. The vestibule organizes the motor activity involved in singing. This is linked to the act of listening carried out by the cochlea. The process begins with assuming a listening posture to which the singing posture will be added.

But first we need to discuss singing in the context of communication systems. All communication entails a speaker and a listener. When the listener replies, he becomes the speaker and the speaker becomes the listener. As soon as either one of the two decides to enter the dialogue, there is an element of control, allowing that person to monitor himself. Consequently, the speaker is the first listener of his own speech. In fact, upon deciding to speak, his brain activates phonation so that a message can be emitted. Control is activated simultaneously, regulating different parameters such as intensity, timber, articulation, attack and release of sounds, the melody of the phrase, and the choice of words. Every aspect of language is monitored in this way, and with singing there is even greater control. This control resides in the ear, where three pathways insure this function.

In reality, we are describing three circuits, two of which arise in the larynx. The first and best circuit is bone conduction. The second circuit, air conduction, relies on muscles and tendons. It gives poor results, and you must avoid using it. By knowing the various loops, you can understand the mechanics of phonation. The two channels you will be using are the internal bone conduction circuit and the external mouth circuit. Each has a completely separate role and the use of each is entirely distinct. The first controls the voice and the second controls articulation. The second depends on the first. Without bone conduction, there is no emission, even if articulation is good.

The mouth circuit does not permit good control over phonation because of its anatomy. Any sound emitted is always complex. It contains a fundamental tone and an associated gamut of harmonics. Once it is launched into the air, the sound is dispersed and no longer subject to control. The high partials travel in a straight line. This effect is even more pronounced at higher pitches, also called directional. The low frequencies, contained in all sounds that are emitted, expand in a circle, bathing the outside of the ear. So when we hear ourselves, we hear a preponderance of lows.

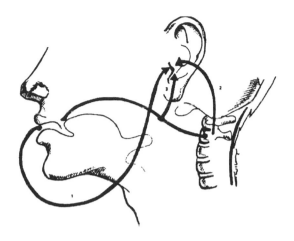

Figure 10.1 Auditory-Vocal Loops

1. From the mouth to the external ear through the auricle
or pavilion. 2. From the larynx to the cervical spine to the
ear. 3. From the mouth through the muscles and tendons
to the ear. Ultimate control resides in the inner ear.

When we listen to our own voice on a recording, we are always surprised to
hear how we sound. While making sounds in a room with good reverberation,
the feedback we get allows us to control high and medium frequencies as well as
lows (see fig. 10.2). This is an example of cybernetic control. Singing obeys the
same laws of regulation and hearing becomes listening.

The Control Loops

All regulation requires the installation of a cybernetic loop. When we are deal-
ing with physiological mechanisms, there has to be an organ of command and
the relays responding to the commands of that central organ. Finally, there is a
control center that oversees whether the emission conforms to the requirements
of the commanding organ. In this case, the different elements are the brain, the
nerves that activate various muscle groups, and nerves that return sensory mes-
sages to the brain, confirming a level of proprioceptive control. The auditory
control collects and coordinates information from the sensory areas. It organizes
whatever it receives through air conduction and bone conduction.

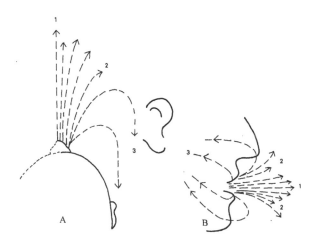

Figure 10.2 Production and Distribution of Frequencies

A: From above. B: Profile.
1. Highs. 2. Mediums. 3. Lows.

The brain, the nervous system with all the peripheral nerves both motor and sensory, the muscles used for singing, and the ear are all connected. This makes it possible to regulate singing and bring it to its highest level. The ear follows the same laws. As you already know from the previous chapter, its anatomy is divided into two blocks, one regulated by the seventh cranial nerve, the other controlled by the trigeminal or fifth cranial nerve. The control of each circuit depends on its own mechanisms. We can observe the following regulatory circuits.

The Audio-Facial Loop

The facial muscles are involved in both the processes of listening and singing. There will be a fuller description of this in the chapter on the listening posture. Both register and intensity affect facial movements, and every tension exerted on the stirrup is accompanied by a facial gesture and vice versa. In the higher registers, the face takes on a very special expression, a grimace. The levator muscles, which are common to the upper lip and the nostrils, contract to close the nose. Motor regulation is carried out by the motor nerve fibers of the facial nerve or the seventh cranial pair, which also innervates the muscles of the stirrup. The sensory regulation responds to a branch of the trigeminal nerve, or the fifth cranial pair. The relationships between these cranial nerves are illustrated in

figure 10.3 which includes the diagrammatic representation of the course of the
facial nerve on the face itself. Note the large area of the face which is controlled
by the nerve, from above the eyes to below the lower lip.

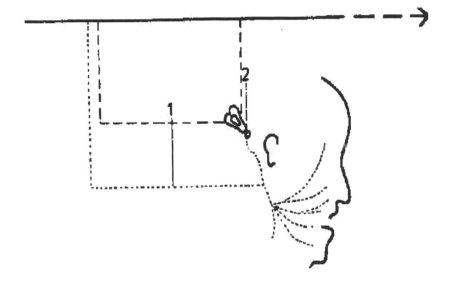

Figure 10.3 Audio-Facial Loop

1. Facial nerve (seventh cranial pair).
2. Stirrup.

The Audio-Mandibular Loop

The mandible is closed or flexed by the chewing muscles. It is opened or extended by the anterior belly of the digastric muscle. Two cranial nerves partici-
pate in this opening and closing: the fifth and seventh. The temporal muscle and
masseter, both flexors, respond to the inferior maxillary nerve, a branch of the
fifth cranial pair (see fig. 10.4). The digastric muscle, the extensor, depends on
the seventh cranial nerve.

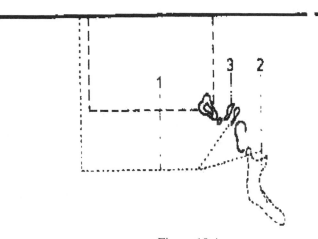

Figure 10.4
Audio-Mandibular Loop

1. Lower maxillary nerve (a branch of the fifth pair).
2. Mandible. 3. Stirrup-hammer combination.

The entire regulation of the ear takes place in the very same neural areas. There is a well-modulated dialogue between the flexor and the extensor muscles. Each adaptive structure of the auditory system is associated to a corresponding structure in the facial mask. The tensions of the muscles of the mandible during articulation are also associated with this regulatory loop, which the ear controls.

The Audio-Larynx Loop

The larynx sets up its own regulation. The ear-larynx loop is one of the most important since sound originates in the larynx. All other vocal regulation depends on this primary regulatory function. The larynx plays a primary role in singing by generating sound (see fig. 10.5). It vibrates and transmits this initial vibration to the entire body, which resonates with it and adds its own frequencies responding specifically to bone structure. Consequently, the whole skeleton sings.

The larynx imprints the basic sound. It furnishes the fundamentals or formants. The body adds the rest, particularly the timber that determines the quality of the voice. The artist who is a virtuoso of his body instrument adds complementary characteristics such as color, inflection, and various other modulations. Singing is not just hitting a note any more than tinkling away on the piano makes you an interpreter. A piano cannot resonate without strings; it would be silent. The same is true of the human body which vibrates with difficulty when the larynx is removed. Even though the esophagus can be used as a substitute, it is impossible to make sounds identical to those resulting from laryngeal activity.

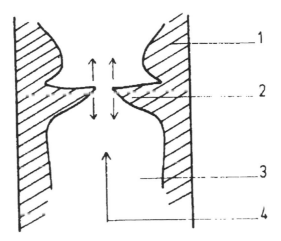

Figure 10.5 Larynx

1. Ventricular bands or false cords. 2. Lower vocal cords.
3. Trachea. 4. Puff of breath.

The larynx is a musculo-cartillagineous organ that sits at the top of the trachea. Although we can identify two sets of vocal cords, only the lower two are involved in singing. The upper cords are commonly called ventricular bands or false vocal cords.

The two lower vocal cords are drawn together and vibrate throughout emission. The vibration is caused by air passing across the cords. The volume of air is so small that it seems almost spontaneous and automatic as with speech. The brain essentially regulates the tension of the vocal cords to keep the flow of air at a minimum, so that the vibration corresponds to the desired pitch.

Many schools have elaborated different theories regarding phonation. However interesting these theories and their applications may be, they do not have any effect on emission. It does not help you as a singer to know whether your vocal cords vibrate on their own or a larynx-lung relationship sets them in motion. I believe that the mechanism that operates in singing is a combination of a subtle exhalation of breath flow and laryngeal tension orchestrated by the brain. The chapter on breathing will expand on this.

The larynx is the major organ of sound emission. Sound produced in the larynx is immediately controlled by the ear. Two circuits are at work, one through bone conduction, the other through air conduction. These circuits meet in the ear, which can absorb both kinds of information, one dedicated to articulation of consonants or words, the second essentially concerned with phonation of vowel sounds. More important for us, the ear-larynx loop permits the regulation of audio-vocal reactions. Figure 10.6 below describes the work of the auditory-phonatory circuit.

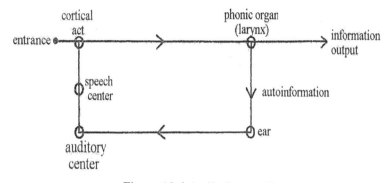

Figure 10.6 Audio-Larynx Loop

The entry point to this cybernetic loop is the intention to sing. This decision sends an impulse to the organs of phonation, especially the larynx. The exit point, shown in figure 10.6, is where the system emits the sound. However, part of the acoustic energy released is assigned to the organ of control, the ear. Its purpose is to send the information to the auditory centers in the brain that control phonation. The return impulse then produces singing.

When I described the audio-laryngeal loop in 1946-1947, I was using cybernetics without knowing it. Cybernetic science officially began with Norbert Wiener in the United States in 1949. All my subsequent work has been based on the discovery of this loop, which I have stated as a law: *"The voice only contains what the ear can hear."* This statement applies exclusively to the right ear; there are no exceptions.

The Audio-Pharyngeal Loop

The pharynx sits on the top of the larynx like a vast funnel and is joined to the nasal faucae in the high anterior portion. Its phonatory activity is intimately connected with that of the larynx and its action is primarily adaptive. That is, it must continuously accommodate to the laryngeal mechanisms, making structural modifications in order to agree with the larynx as it moves. In precise acoustic terms, this requires an adaptation of impedance. Everything that is generated in the larynx is facilitated and maintained through a group of adaptive processes.

This is an automatic adaptation that must be allowed to take place. The objective for both the pharynx and the larynx is to keep the throat open and supple, avoiding closure by the constrictor muscles. The regulation of the pharynx under the organizing control of the ear consists of achieving what is famous in singing as the open throat with the help of the dilator muscles and the tongue.

The ear assumes many regulatory functions, including that of the ascendant vestibulo-mesoencephalic fasciculum which flows into the longitudinal posterior fasciculum and rejoins, among others, the glossopharyngeal nerve or the ninth cranial pair. These regulatory centers simultaneously control the ninth cranial pair for the pharynx, the tenth cranial pair for the larynx, and the twelfth cranial pair for the tongue, making it possible for these nerves to operate in close association.

The Audio-Lingual Loop

During singing, the tongue responds to the demands of the ear in two ways. First, it forms the anterior surface of the pharynx and must take a position that does not interfere with the opening of the pharynx. Second, it has to attain certain positions which are central to singing. The audio-lingual loop also includes the ear-brain circuit, and the twelfth cranial pair. The original purpose of the tongue and its seventeen muscles is to help with swallowing. It became involved in phonation because of the regulation that we are describing in figure 10.7.

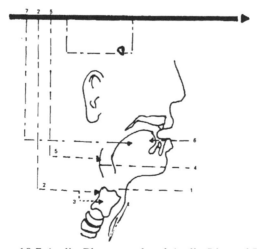

Figure 10.7 Audio-Pharyngeal and Audio-Lingual Loop

1. Larynx. 2. Pneumogastric or vagus nerve (tenth pair).
3. Recurrent nerves. 4. Pharynx. 5. Glossopharyngeal nerve (ninth pair). 6. Tongue. 7. Hypoglossal nerve (twelfth pair).

The ear's influence is, as always, critical. When electronic filters provide the ear with vigilant listening, the tongue takes the position most favorable for emission. More information on that subject will be found in part three. The tongue has a very important role in singing, and mastery of its movements is difficult to attain.

The Audio-Thoracic Loop

The thorax contains the lungs, which play an important role in singing. They act as a motor, diffusing the air in a specific way, their function closely tied to that of the thorax. The thorax is bounded at the base by the diaphragm, a powerful, muscular plateau that divides the trunk into two parts, with the thorax above and the abdomen below. The thorax is limited at the sides by the rib cage, which attaches at the sternum in front, except for the lowest ribs, which insert into the vertebrae at the rear, but have no solid connection in front and are therefore called floating ribs. The clavicles sit atop the ribs in the front of the thorax, while the shoulder blades are seated in the upper part of the thorax to the rear, on the right and left. This whole apparatus involves a number of muscles that can widen this enormous container when it fills, while other muscles empty it.

We will detail all the regulatory loops directing the muscles of the thoracic cage: the pectorals, the larger latissimus dorsalis, the intercostals, and the circuits of the diaphragm. Beginning with the brain and under constant cochleo-vestibular (inner ear) monitoring, a collection of loops is found throughout the vestibular-mesoencephalic fasciculum and the posterior longitudinal band. These regulate the anterior cervical muscles as well as the upper part of the back and the diaphragm. The brachial plexus controls the pectoral muscles innervated by the intercostal nerves. The phrenic nerve disperses in the direction of the diaphragm.

Here, more than in any other loop, cooperation with the larynx is essential because breath control depends on the gentlest possible flow of air through the larynx. This is difficult to apportion, yet the unconstrained functioning of the larynx absolutely depends upon the mastery of this airflow.

The Audio-Mouth and the Audio-Nasal Loops

Discussion of the mouth and the nasal faucae has intentionally been omitted. Their effect is important, potentially causing, in the case of the mouth, over-articulation and in the case of the nasal faucae, over-phonation. The functions of both the mouth and the nasal faucae depend upon the adept regulation of the tongue, the muscles of mastication, and the facial muscles. The muscles of the lips and the wings of the nose form part of a muscular group controlled by the loops corresponding to the fifth, seventh, and twelfth cranial pairs.

The Audio-Recurrential Loop

The vagus nerve or tenth cranial pair regulates numerous loops by itself. For singing, the most important regulation is that of the larynx. This is carried out through the recurrent nerves, both the right and left, which are asymmetrical in their return trajectory towards the larynx. The ear-larynx loop is likewise vital. A study of the recurrent nerves will clarify these mechanisms.

In figure 10.8, you can see an anatomical difference: the right branch of the recurrent nerve is shorter than the left. Note that after separating from the vagus nerve, the right recurrent branch makes a loop around the subclavian artery, while the left recurrent branch goes around the aorta itself, making a loop that is both longer and lower. The neuro-motor regulations arising from this organization explain certain phenomena: the systematic repetitions found in the babbling of babies and in stuttering. Both occur when the right branch has not achieved complete dominance over the left. This also explains why some people use what I call a right voice or a left voice, depending upon which branch is preferred for speaking. This anatomical asymmetry sets up the process of lateralization so important in speech and singing. It leads the two hemispheres of the brain to function at slightly different speeds, because the right recurrent is shorter than the left. This asymmetry has enormous influence over language and over gesture.

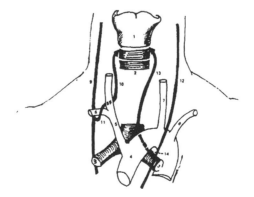

Figure 10.8 The Two Recurrent Nerves

1. Larynx. 2. Trachea. 3. Bronchial tube. 4. Aorta. 5. Right common carotid artery. 6. Right subclavian artery. 7. Left carotid artery. 8. Left subclavian artery. 9. Right vagus nerve (tenth pair). 10. Right recurrent nerve. 11. Subclavian artery. 12. Left pneumogastric nerve. 13. Left recurrent nerve. 14. Sub-aortic loop.

It is absolutely essential to know about the recurrent nerves, the motor nerves of the larynx, if we want to understand how the larynx functions. The study of the asymmetry of these two branches as it applies to other fields is beyond the purpose of this book. In my opinion, however, the right recurrent nerve is the most essential element of the audio-vocal loop. This loop, starting with the brain, assumes all the commands that determine the quality of singing and operates under the control of the right ear. The recurrent nerve is the only one that has fibers with three different conduction speeds.

The Audio-Lumbar-Sacral Loop

As we already know, the vestibule controls body posture and to sing well, we need good posture: the pelvis must be rotated forward. The lumbar curve diminishes under the direction of the lumbar and sacral nerve roots.

The Audio-Cervical Loop

As soon as the effect of an action is felt in the sacrum, there is a response in the back of the neck. The cervical curve is further minimized when the lumbar curve disappears, and vice versa. These reactions take place under cochleo-vestibular supervision.

The Audio-Corporeal Loops

The entire body must be taken into account in singing. Every part of the body remains active during excellent performance. The body, set in motion by the skeleton, resonates like a vibrant torch. The entire bone structure is involved: the spine reinforces and disburses the sounds produced by the vocal cords. The link between the ear and the body is powerfully orchestrated by auditory control. The mechanics of regulation have been so vigorously emphasized to convince you that one sings with one's ear and more specifically with only the right ear. Now it is time to integrate this information with the practice of singing.

Maria Callas was the only singer who came to my office announcing that she could no longer control her singing with her right ear. Most people are not so keenly aware of their ears and the relationship of listening to control. I told her she would need at least three months of training to correct the situation. Unfortunately, she was afraid to renege on a trip she had planned on the yacht of Aristotle Onassis, so she never did the training.

PART III

VOCAL TECHNIQUE

CHAPTER 11

HOW TO SING

Vocal technique must involve both the ear and the singing voice in order to be effective. Part three deals with the training necessary to achieve this. To become a virtuoso requires intense work, first to acquire the basics, and then to polish your technique until it shines.

The singer is one of the most complex structures imaginable for making music. You are both virtuoso and musical instrument. Each part of the body involved in singing needs to be isolated, trained, and then integrated as a functioning whole. Your margin for error is slimmer than that of an instrumentalist. A voice can be repaired to a point but you certainly can't buy a new one.

An instrumentalist's preparation of a new piece is pretty straightforward. With practice he gradually establishes his neuro-sensory and neuro-muscular circuits required for performance. He will need to repeat difficult passages more often. In general the score is practiced with the intensity, nuances, and speed indicated in the score as close as possible to performance level. Many people believe that singers should practice as though they were instrumentalists and put their music "in voice." The following story will illustrate what happens when you do.

For many years I worked with a singer who had a first-class instrument. The Paris Opera staged productions especially chosen to showcase her talent. She was the picture of vocal health with a gorgeous sound, so precise in pitch and nuance that it transported audiences. She was absolutely brilliant. Her singing transmitted a feeling of serene joy.

Eventually, however, she got into vocal trouble. How could that have happened? Unfortunately, she fell into the clutches of an accompanist who was impossibly demanding. Every singer at the Paris Opera had to receive his stamp of approval before being pronounced ready to go on stage. He made them put entire roles in voice. Although he was particularly insightful musically, he couldn't resist meddling with vocal technique. Still worse, for him, "getting ready" meant practicing at full voice for hours on end in a tiny rehearsal room. Singing that loud in a confined space will damage the ear through excessively intense reverberation. Singing at performance level must be reserved for spaces big enough to allow the sound to disperse, preferably the stage.

He was forever on her back, so our singer was in grave danger and she was stuck with him: he was her husband! He made her sing music that she knew backwards and forwards, at full voice. Taxed beyond endurance, she developed professional deafness from her own voice in cramped quarters. She ran from one ENT to another but her throat problems were secondary to the loss of auditory control of her high notes. With her ear no longer able to control her singing, her larynx began to malfunction.

I warned her. I even met with her husband several times to explain to him what was happening. He pretended to agree with me but continued to do as he pleased. Of course, by being so stubborn he also subjected himself to a steady stream of operatic voices blasting away in his little practice room. You have to wonder how his own ears fared.

Numerous singers got into vocal trouble thanks to him. Not doubt they found ways to avoid him. But his own wife! It took only a few years for her to crash and burn. As a result, many titles staged expressly for her had to be withdrawn. I wish I could say that this was an unusual case, but unfortunately destructive coaches are all too common.

Vocal training must be carried out judiciously. You need to have new music in your ear before you start to sing it. Do not make the mistake of trying to sing before you know all the notes.

My father, who was expert at conserving his voice, used to say you only have so many high notes and you better use them wisely. He disapproved of singers who honked away all day long and had nothing left for the stage. No actor taxes his endurance by endlessly declaiming his monologues and neither should you. Although it takes daily training to become an excellent singer, you should never vocalize for more than an hour and a half in thirty-minute periods each over the course of the day.

We must distinguish between the responsibilities of the singing teacher and those of coach-accompanists. A good singing teacher will train his student in every aspect of vocal technique, and teach the student to harmonize all the elements so that none is exaggerated. Once the student can make good sounds the teacher will guide him in interpretation.

The coach-accompanist, who is not trained in the voice, must limit his comments to interpretation and style. He has no business giving technical advice beyond noting that there is work to be done in a specific area. Every singer, no matter how accomplished, will need guidance in matters of taste from time to time.

Bear in mind the many systems involved in feeding and supporting sound as you continue to read. Relating to the human body as a musical instrument is a tall order, but if you can be precise in your use of physiological terms specific to the act of singing, you and your teacher will have a common language to use in the learning process.

Teaching voice relies on subjective sensations that can only be described in words. Clearly, it is important that this structure be precise and appropriate. Deepening your understanding of the vocal gesture will help you to clarify your technical goals. The teacher who wishes to make effective observations and guide the student must know how to sing and demonstrate well.

Physiological terminology gives you a way to avoid the use of vague and confusing metaphors. We have to make our sensations conscious so that they can they be reproduced at will and associated to the corresponding muscular response. Singing is a natural act that is superimposed on all other bodily activities. To begin this process, we have to take organs whose basic purposes are other than those we intend in singing, and tame them for our purposes. The hallmark of a high degree of mastery is that the spectator will not distinguish between the technical and musical elements of a performance.

Singing appears to have developed in response to a profound need to give expression to thoughts and feelings. It is intentions, inflections, and emotional meanings that make a long apprenticeship and daily practice indispensable to maintaining and refining this very specific way of singing words.

I invite you to rethink the functional structure of singing described in Part II as we go through the different aspects of using the body to sing. A well-defined body image specific to the act of singing implies a well organized mental attitude and finely tuned alignment, which will allow the entire body to resonate during singing.

Now that you know that the right ear controls singing, and you can observe the right side of the face is more active during the process, let me say that to exaggerate this will not help you. Do not get into the habit of trying to make the right side of your face more active and do not get into the habit of cupping your hand around your right ear. This is an exaggeration that will not help you develop normal control.

Once the listening posture has been well defined, we will move on to the action of sound resonance in the living, vibrating body-instrument. Laryngeal control, the dosing of breath that accompanies it, and the emission of the vowels will all be touched on in the chapters that follow.

CHAPTER 12

LISTENING POSTURE: EAR AND BODY

Efficient body alignment activates listening and the listening posture in the ear is central to singing. The way we stand and move calls upon every part of our being and mobilizes the brain and every circuit of the nervous system, to and from the brain, both motor and sensory. It is a remarkable assemblage of cells living out an amazing communication process as it distributes information to and returns it from the various parts of the body. This dynamic employs two energetic processes: one is a metabolic process for nutrition and oxygenation; the other is a physical-chemical process arising from complex stimuli.

Insufficient stimulation of the brain has been shown to result in serious damage and we now know the how much stimulation is necessary for good functioning of the nervous system. The ear processes most of this stimulation, and is the principal generator of cortical energy.

We know that the vestibule processes the stimulation of every muscle in the body and sends information to regulate upright posture, mobility, and body movements. Impulses toward erect posture, muscle tone, and movement create responses, in the form of information and stimulation emanating from the muscles, tendons, joints, and even from the bones. This enormous excitation alone accounts for the increased tone that leads to movement, good balance, and good posture.

The easier it is to stand correctly, the easier it is to maintain posture. There is a self-regulatory mechanism which begins to operate automatically as soon as the ear's various organs, the utricle and its semi-circular canals, the saccule and the cochlea, move into place in the embryo, thereby setting the stage for the listening posture. This complex control circuit arises in the vestibule and disseminates throughout the body, preparing it to receive energy while conferring balance, upright posture, and the ability to perfect movement, moment by moment. It rectifies, compensates, and balances all movements so as to harmonize and integrate them with the global body dynamic.

The listening faculty requires optimal hearing to control the whole ear, both vestibule and cochlea. When the vestibule orients itself in space to the position that allows it to take control over the body, listening can be at its best, so for our purposes posture in both the ear and the body are of paramount importance.

The vestibule produces an enormous flow of stimuli, feeding the cerebral cortex with information received through its connections to the muscles and joints and to its action over the entire skeleton. When it is functioning well the cochlea also adds important stimulation central to listening. Its job is to make sure that the vestibule assumes an adequate posture. It contributes to the determination of the kind of vertical stance required for listening, and invites the whole body to function at optimal level so that we can listen well.

Even the surface of the skin takes part in this dynamic activation. In the embryo it evolves out of the neural tube, along with the rest of the developing nervous system. The skin is richly supplied with sensory receptors, principally in the face, the anterior part of the thorax, the abdomen, the inside of the arms, the palms of the hand, the inside of the thighs and the legs, as well as the soles of the feet. These places interpret pressures made on the skin by sound waves, even when they are below the threshold of conscious awareness. So it makes sense when someone doesn't want to listen he may turn his back or step aside, so that he presents the parts of his body that has fewer sound receptors.

The vestibule regulates posture; there is a second regulator: the communication process. When one person speaks to another, the listener is made to experience the same proprioceptive sensations as the speaker and frequently the listener models his body posture on that of the speaker. When the listener resonates in his body, his posture and his verticality are affected and he opens himself up to receive the speaker's words. The entire peripheral nervous system, both afferent and efferent, galvanizes. The information it sends sparks sensory responses towards the central nervous system, and involves the whole organism, including the cerebral cortex itself.

The cochlea stimulates virtually the entire brain, while the vestibule controls the rest of the motor and sensory nervous system. In order to listen, the cochlea must summon the vestibule to position the body so it can receive the maximum amount of stimulation through postural responses, including the energy supplied by resistance to gravity and the presentation of sound receptors in the skin on the front of the body, etc.

Sounds are differentiated in the cochlear duct or organ of Corti. Each frequency is perceived in its own assigned location along the duct, where it distributes to the hair cells, which are specialized according to pitch. Then they are sent towards the cerebral cortex. The same localized differentiation is observed on the left temporal lobe, where the auditory area is located. This temporal area is very important for memory and concentration. It is divided into three zones.

This is the area of nominative memory, especially important in singing. Information disseminated to the entire encephalon through the fascia originates in the preceding area, flows in the direction of the pontine nuclei and thence to the cerebellum. We now understand the importance of such a network for all the circuits controlling the audio-vocal mechanism.

The most important facts to remember:
- The ear brings about the listening posture,
- The ideal stance for vocal emission depends on this posture,
- This somatic-corporal structure results from a perpetual dialogue between the vestibule and the cochlea,
- These two structures, both part of the labyrinth, develop early to prepare for the listening posture and, at the same time, work together to provide an optimally energized encephalon through stimulation.

Sounds collected in the inner ear impact the entire labyrinth. The vestibule uses sounds, preparing the body to adjust its posture for listening. The cochlea breaks sounds into their various elements and sends its analysis to the brain, thus extending its reach throughout the nervous system. The brain begins the process of differentiating the frequencies and sending them to pitch receptors. Then, after gathering in the temporal cortex, they are distributed throughout the most recent part of the brain. Finally, the entire information is redistributed to the whole body.

In other words, a conversation is begun between the vestibule and the cochlea simultaneously with the dialogue between the cortex and the body. All information decoded in the cochlea and transferred to the cortex is made part of the body as a result of the communication between the vestibule and cochlea. That information is also incorporated through the connections linking the cortex to the body's motor nerves, which are closely associated to the fascia emanating from the vestibule.

The connection between the ear and the body is further strengthened because it is built into the structure of the ear and the nervous system, which depends heavily upon the ear. All regulatory mechanisms are acquired and made fully operational as a result of the dialogue between the ear and the nervous system.

The listening posture requires that the spinal column be well aligned and standing tall along its vertical axis following its natural curves. The vestibule, which has command over every muscle of the body, brings about this erect stance by means of:

1. The vestibulo-spinal tract, both ipse- and contra-lateral and
2. The vestibular-mesoencephalic tract, again both ipse- and contra-lateral.

The sensory responses following the return tracts complete the control of the whole body (see: integrators, figs. 9.1, 9.2, 9.3).

To sum up, the vestibule demands a certain posture of the body in order to enhance listening; moreover, the cochlea forces the vestibule to adopt that posture. In the dialogue between the cochlea and vestibule, the vestibule follows the directives of the cochlea to achieve the best possible posture for efficient listening.

The erect body posture indispensable to finely tuned listening must be accompanied by good posture in the ear itself. What does this mean? Can we really talk about a posture of the ear the same way we do about body posture? Yes, absolutely. Remember that the middle ear has two muscles that use tension to regulate the auditory response curve. It is the inner ear that regulates hearing, and its mechanisms are closely tied to the adaptive responses of the middle ear.

Consider this analogy for a moment. Just as the retina is the sensory organ of vision, the hair cells of the organ of Corti are the sensory apparatus of hearing. In the eye, the iris adapts to light and the lens accommodates to sight, but the retina can only see if the eyelids are opened. The organ of Corti will be used in the same manner if the middle ear knows how to adapt to intensity and to accommodate to the frequency spectrum. The muscles of the hammer and the stirrup, along with the regulatory mechanics of the eustachian tube, organize all the operations, which lead to good listening. It has an impact on listening as profound as that of opening the eyelid has on vision.

Depending upon their tension, the muscles of the hammer and stirrup totally modify the auditory response curve. It is as if the desire to listen shapes the curve. The psyche and openness to the outside world interact through the ear. In truth, this phenomenon applies to all sensory organs but it is with audition that the impact here is the most remarkable. The mind impacts audition and the ear impacts the mind. It is clear that the ear will have an effect over the voice.

How to Practice the Listening Posture

A person whose listening ability is excellent will have good posture. Anyone less adept at listening will have to make an effort to attain it. Achieving the listening posture requires mastering the tension of the muscles of both the stirrup and the hammer, since they form a cybernetic regulatory system that directs the inner ear and adjusts the tension of the eardrum. Audio-vocal education, with the aid of modern electronics, which I developed for this purpose, is extremely efficient in speeding up the process of acquiring excellent listening.

Hearing is a superficial use of one's ear, while listening implies an act of will to connect with the sonic environment and learn what must be known. It is through the listening posture that we make the shift from a passive awareness that there is some sort of sound, to listening: paying attention to the sound and becoming actively involved with it.

How Do You Acquire this Posture?

Sit comfortably the edge of a table or a stool, high enough to allow the legs to dangle. Close your eyes and allow the head to seek the position of balance. It will hang slightly forward because the vestibule searches for the horizontal plane of the head through the lower surface of the utricle. This parallels an imaginary horizontal plane that runs through the lower border of your closed upper eyelid and connects with the opening of the right auditory canal. In that position, the highest point of the head is situated at its true vertex.

(If you were to lift your head the way a bird does when you sing, you will hear badly. The highs are broken and you will have to push to make a sound, and even if it sounds good, it will shorten your career.)

Now search out the high frequency sounds among all the other sounds in the environment. To do this you have to play with the muscles of the middle ear. How do you do that? Begin by imagining that the whole scalp pulls back as if you wanted to make a tight, dense ponytail at the back of your head, near the vertex. When you do this, the horizontal lines on the forehead will tend to disappear. It is a bit like wiggling your ears, if you ever tried that as a kid. You will feel a very clear sensation at the scalp line as you smooth out your forehead, and a cool sensation will spread across your brow. It only takes a few moments to acquire and maintain this position.

Now you are ready to widen the skin of the forehead as much as possible as if you wanted it to touch the walls of the room. After several moments, feel as if you were pulling the skin of the forehead back to become part of that little ponytail behind the vertex. Pull strongly so the skin is well stretched and be careful not to raise the head. Keep the horizontal line between eyelid and the opening of the right ear canal. Now any vertical creases in the forehead, especially in the middle, will disappear. The forehead becomes broad and smooth.

You will know when you have mastered this second step because your face will flush and then grow pale. At the same time, you will notice that your breath becomes profound, quiet, and regular and acquires an unusual amplitude and rhythm. That is the way breathing feels when it is natural and free.

When the skin is pulled back this way, you will notice that the upper lids close naturally, as a result of their own weight. You will not have to hold them closed. You may feel a slight trembling of the eyelids at the sides of the orbits. Then try to stretch the skin under the eyes out toward the sides of the room. The face relaxes, wrinkles fade.

Once more pull the facial muscles back into the little buns as tightly as you can. Everything is pulled toward the bun. The upper portion of the visible part of the ear (the auricle) is also pulled toward the little bun. You are actually treating yourself to a "physiological face-lift." As you keep doing this, you may even see your face start to look better.

Now that you can pull all the muscles of the face toward the back, let the upper lip rest on the lower lip, as a capital on a column, in a tranquil half-smile indicating that there is balance between the orbicular muscles, which circle the mouth and the muscles at the corners of the mouth. As a result of this balance, the lower jaw is in contact with the upper jaw without any tension. These efforts give the face an unusually relaxed and rested appearance, without lines and hollows.

It is important to learn to keep this peaceful face and relaxed mouth while staying alive to the environment. You will notice that sounds become purer; they take on a clear, luminous timbre. The lows fade as you become more aware of the higher harmonics they contain. The surroundings assume a radiant, live, and vibrant color.

Once you can listen for highs, which won't take long, you have to find your real voice the same way, by seeking the high harmonics. This is very subtle, and when you begin to perceive the voice this way, it is an entirely new experience. It feels as if you are far away from yourself with your right ear leading until you feel your sound emanating from a point located just behind the vertex in the same place as our little bun.

From a physiological point of view, this place is called the point of fusion (the crown of the head). Just imagine your perception of sound gliding along an axis that runs from the nostrils to the point of fusion. The perception of sound seems to get further away from this point at the same time that it appears to get wider. It will quickly move a distance of several fractions of an inch, then several yards to finally settle some distance away. This is, of course, an impression, but one deeply felt.

The idea is to listen to your own voice as if from far away so that you could preserve this as a reference point from which to view yourself and others objectively. When we listen this way, it feels as if the song and the words pass through us, as though we were channeling the music. There is nothing so liberating as to abandon oneself to this process.

CHAPTER 13

BONE CONDUCTION

We have come to one of the most important points in the art of singing: making the most of bone conduction so that the entire skeleton sings along with the balanced vibration of the larynx. It is as if the singer has a voice in his bones. In Part II, I described how sound transmits through the air, and through bone. I will review the basics of the neurophysiology of singing and tell you how to achieve bone conduction.

After you learn how to stand straight and get the kind of muscle tone you need, your voice will acquire the resonance in the bones that is the mark of a great singer. Good posture reduces the impact of gravity, allowing muscles to work more efficiently. In the vertical position, the trunk is erect, the thorax wide open. The actions of the cochlea over the vestibule, the vestibule over the body, and the body over the muscle tone develop an entirely new postural profile.

This posture has an enormous effect on vocal emission. Standing straight arranges the body so that the spine lengthens. The enormous ligament of Bertin connects the pelvis with the head of the femur. You may need to work on it to have a strong straight spine. When you stand straight and tall (see fig. 13.1), the back of the larynx comes closer to the front of the cervical spine. The diaphragm moves down and the esophagus follows because they are connected. The muscles and ligaments form the vertebrae into a balanced structure. The spinal column is free to vibrate when the larynx excites it because, in this position, it is completely unencumbered. The larynx completely changes its dynamic of emission, in this position.

When the larynx is in a bad position (see fig. 13.2), it does indeed act like the mouthpiece of a wind instrument, trying to activate the structures below. In singing posture, the larynx sends resonance to the bones that touch it. The spinal column then sets all structures that touch it into resonance. Once the bones begin to sing, they cause the cavities to vibrate. The voice becomes vibrant, and more harmonious. It is the resonance emanating from every bone in the body that causes this change.

How do we make the larynx operate autonomously? Good singing gives you the control to leave the larynx and the breathing apparatus alone, so they can work together with the greatest possible ease. If we get out of the way of normal physiological mechanisms, the larynx creates its own ideal conditions. The cords have just the right tension when the larynx is free to move along the cervical spine.

Anyone who violently pushes on the larynx to make it go lower or higher is being overzealous. The result is a contrived emission and it might seem that the larynx has a complex job and that singing entails a lot of muscular activity. Many singers who believe in muscular strength push violently against their larynxes. Certainly no good singer would do that. Unnecessary effort causes disharmony. The larynx moves around and makes accommodations automatically, needing only the vigilant control of the right ear. How does this automatic activity operate? Remember that every muscle in the body, and that includes the larynx, is under the control of the labyrinth. So it is the vestibulo-mesoencephalic bundles that act to regulate the motor bundles of the pneumogastric nerve.

Figure 13.1 Correct Posture.   Figure 13.2 Incorrect Posture.

In correct emission, the larynx is lined up against the cervical spine, which, excited by the vibrations transmitted to the larynx by the vocal cords, starts to sing of its own accord. Under these circumstances, the larynx is excited exactly as the strings of a violin. It is the strings that vibrate and the violin that sings. When the posture of the singer is well aligned, his larynx excites the vertebral column, just as if it were that little piece of wood inside the violin that is call the "soul" of the violin. Its purpose is to carry sound from the anterior plate of the violin to the posterior plate.

The Larynx as Tuning Fork

How does the cervical spine start to resonate? It is a law that when one vibrating object comes into contact with another, the second object will start vibrating of its own accord. The way the second object is set in motion is determined by the acoustic phenomena that result from its own physical structure.

A tuning fork that has been set in motion vibrates at its own frequency, determined by its length and the thickness of its branches. When it is placed into contact with a crystal goblet, two things happen. The tuning fork will continue to vibrate, and as soon as it touches the crystal it too will vibrate with its own characteristic sound. The two resonances will blend. The same thing happens with the spinal column. It starts to sing under the effect of the vibration of the larynx, which is a real tuning fork resting on the cervical spine. (Of course there is tissue between the larynx and the spine, just as there is tissue over your bones when the doctor uses a tuning fork and the bone rings).

Laryngeal vibrations form fundamental tones, while the harmonic shower of sparks associated with the fundamentals, rich in higher frequencies and reinforcing the initial sound considerably, depend on the skeleton. There are many advantages to the activation of this bony resonance. The energy that is dispensed is extremely important. Ample, warm, dense sounds are made with minimum effort. Because of this activation and the special ability of the skeleton to transmit sounds, the control adopted by the bony voice is direct, conserves energy, and maintains the integrity of the full spectrum of sound. This production has nothing in common with ordinary vocal emission, even if that emission sounds easy.

This degree of control is difficult, if not impossible, when we use only air conduction. Bone filters for higher sounds at the expense of lows, making sounds that are particularly rich and dense. To get an idea of the sound that is generated, think of Caruso. He had a colossal output of energy: the gamut of the highs was seven to fourteen times higher than that of the fundamentals. The same was true of Feodor Chaliapin.

It is easy to see the advantages of an emission that is easily controlled and rich in high frequencies. It has a propensity to align the spine. This in turn facilitates emission, releasing progressively more energy. Sounds that vibrate the entire skull stimulate the pineal gland. Scientific opinion is divided as to whether or not this gland is important but it is certainly possible that the creative energy that is unleashed by such sounds may be related to their action over glandular tissue.

If we look at a spectrographic analysis of sounds emitted by bone conduction, we see that they distribute so that the curve, with the exception of fundamentals, produces a profile of ascendant responses that resemble those of the ears' thresholds. You know the role of the cochlea-vestibular apparatus in phonation as well as in posture. Remember that the right ear directs all the other elements of control. Let's look at the reasons why this ear should be accorded a position of such importance in vocal emission.

It is inconceivable that good sound can be maintained for long without control. When good sounds are emitted randomly without auditory control, there is no relationship between the hearing curve and the voiceprint's curve. However, once the sound becomes consistent, denoting a certain mastery of phonation, a parallel, or better yet, a similarity is established, demonstrating the law: *The larynx does not emit what the ear does not control.*

This mastery is especially marked in singers. We can study their technique with voiceprints. By following the response curve that emerges from spectrographic analysis of their voices, we can tell whether their control is achieved through air or through bone conduction. When diagrams contain elevated bands, the sensation of bone conduction has clearly been the means of control. Prints containing fewer high-frequency impulses indicate control based solely on listening to sound returning through the air.

As you may remember, this corresponds to a curve indicating dissemination of a complex sound emanating from a fixed point—in this case, the mouth. Analysis becomes more delicate because the two controls, air and bone, mix together. However, we can tell from the curve what percentage of one or the other is controlling the sound. You can of course get the same information by listening but we all love to see it in black and white.

Just remember that you will get the same results whether you look at the listening curve or listen to the voice. We can prove this experimentally by introducing filters that make frequency cuts. The voice changes that result follow the modifications made to the auditory input, which uses whatever auditory channel remains. These reactions cannot be induced throughout the entire spectrum because there are limits to how far the larynx can follow the sound. However if the upper partials are removed from auditory control, the voice will model itself on the lower band. It gets lower. When the lows are suppressed, you will see the highs light up on the response curve.

You have to stay within the realm of what is possible for people. If you decide to cut all the frequencies up to 6000Hz with a filter that goes from 0 to 6000Hz, it creates a disturbance. Control will be altered and vocal responses will be aberrant, random. However, for 3000Hz and maybe up to as high as 4000Hz, there will be a positive response, but that is the limit. If you cut at 2000Hz using a high-pass filter, you facilitate emission, a durable response that corresponds to the modification. You can clearly observe a reaction, which you will get even more easily when you modify both bone and air conduction. Note that these changes happen only with the right ear.

As a result of the above experiments, I proved the presence of a dominant ear in 1950. Several years later, I was able to prove that only the right ear has this potential for control. Very occasionally you get someone with true left ear dominance, but it will never work as well as dominance of the right ear, as we have seen with the singer in Part I.

Production of Bone Conduction

Now that you know about bone conduction, how do you make it work for you in singing? How do you develop a voice production that permits the entire body to resonate? First, make sure that listening is optimized. Otherwise you will only produce your voice well by chance, and you will feel completely dependent on your voice teacher as a means of control. Through the time-honored method of diligently practicing numerous exercises, these mechanisms will start to operate, provided the ear improves as a result. But it can take a very long time. It is far quicker, easier, and more precise to accomplish this through listening training. Your teacher will thank you for it.

What can we expect from bone conduction? Can we feel something happening? We have to be very careful of what we say about proprioceptive sensations, since they vary so much from one person to another and defy objective criteria. Some people feel sensations between the eyes, others say they are putting their voice in the mask, still others feel it at the top of the head. Each person can tell us what he feels. But his sensations will not be those of others. Always describe objectively how you feel bone conduction and avoid the use of metaphor.

There are several ways to achieve bone conduction. First and foremost, get the sensation through humming. You have to do this correctly to avoid trouble with vocal mechanics. You have to be in listening posture, with the spinal column in its most natural alignment and the head inclined slightly forward, as described above. With the mouth in a closed position, feel your lips resting against each other not clamped shut. Your upper teeth gently resting on the lower teeth, not biting, the tongue in a relaxed position with the front edge and tip gently resting against the closed teeth. Breathe in slowly and gently through the nose without altering the position of the lips, teeth, or tongue. Now try to exhale gently and slowly not allowing any air to exit the nose. This will cause the larynx to rise or fall slightly according to what pitch you have naturally chosen to hum. Do not push the air as this will make a guttural sound and not allow you to feel any vibrating sensation in the mouth, on the lips, or in the facial area. The following examples will allow you to detect how it feels when you are doing it wrong.

Begin humming with your lips closed and allow the lower jaw to drop. Lower the tongue and rest it on the floor of the mouth (see fig. 13.3). This creates a cavity behind the lips, giving rise to a dead, difficult-to-modulate sound of poor quality.

This is not what we are looking for. Try this! Close your mouth with the teeth touching without contracting the muscles in the lower jaw. Just let the teeth barely touch. Notice that the tongue occupies your whole mouth. The point of the tongue touches the incisors, and the back of the tongue rises to rest against the hard palate, without any pressure being exerted. The inside of your mouth will look like figure 13.4.

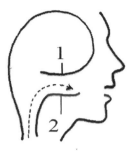

Figure 13.3 Mouth Closed [sic], Sound in the Mouth

1. Hard palate. 2. Tongue.

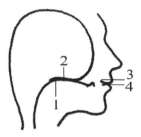

Figure 13.4 Mouth Closed

It is hard to resist the desire to project the sound in front right around the face, in the direction of a listener. This way of thinking is a very strong habit. But if you do it that way, you can no longer use the mouth as a channel, so the hum has no choice but to go into the nose. Now you get a nasal sound, so that's not it either (see fig. 13.5). You can tell the difference between these two ways of humming. If you do it the first way, the mouth resonates with a heavy, dead sound, devoid of "ping." It lacks quality and you won't be able to add harmonics. The second way produces a nasal sound. Even though easier to produce, and you may feel better about it, nasal quality sounds lousy to us. If it is not going to come from the mouth or nose, where will it come from? You make it with the whole body through the excitation of the spinal column and the contact between the larynx and the cervical vertebrae (see fig. 13.6).

Bone conduction has a special timber, rich, heady, and colorful. It has an ethereal quality and seems to come from outside the body. It literally awakens the environment with a smooth, vibrant, and dense sonority. It carries with ease. What is more, when you have it nailed, this sound can be quickly modulated over the entire vocal range without costing you any effort.

It will take a while to get the knack of humming this way, but hang in there. This is the first step towards excellent singing. This should only be practiced on a couple of notes in the middle of the vocal range. You can then extend the range of the hum both upwards and downwards. In extending the exercise, you will encounter something we call the *passaggio*, which asks you to do something different with your voice in order to continue expanding the range. For now just do the exercise as far as you can and still feel comfortable. The comfort level in young untrained voices can sometimes go right "through" the *passaggio* areas, which will cause serious vocal damage later unless rigidly controlled by a competent teacher. Humming should only be done in notes lying easily within the central part of the vocal range. We will cover the *passaggio* in later chapters.

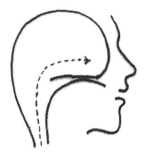

Figure 13.5 Nasal Sound, Mouth Closed [sic]

Make sure you continue in listening posture throughout the exercise. Carrying out the two actions simultaneously does more than prepare for singing; it energizes the brain and the rest of the nervous system through the rich stimulation produced by the action of the vestibule over the body, and the cochlea over the cerebral cortex.

Good bone conduction feeds the nervous system, prompts the larynx to take appropriate positions depending on the register, and allows the singer to become aware of the movement of the pharyngeal walls. The pharynx will start to widen, counteracting its natural tendency toward constriction in swallowing.

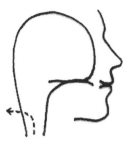

Figure 13.6 Correctly Produced Bone Conduction

I would like to take the opportunity to clear up a misunderstanding. Certain singing teachers have a habit of asking their students to place the voice in the mask. This expression comes in fact from the Greeks who really wore masks on stage as a theatrical device. Singing is something else. When the teacher tells his student to put the voice "in the mask" he is most likely asking him to place his voice in the front, but if you push your sound forward it becomes nasal. In fact it is the whole body that sings, set in resonance through bone conduction. Some people think that you have to exercise this or that resonator in order to make good sounds. You often hear people speak of making the sinuses sing.

Sinuses do not sing. I have had many opportunities to confirm this in my ENT practice. I will give you only two examples. A great singer, very well known, came to me because he had frequent headaches. I asked for an X-ray of his sinuses and was surprised to find that he had no frontal sinuses. However he had a beautiful voice, and well placed.

Another world-famous singer used to come to my office when he was in France because he suffered from a rather serious sinusitis. Even though his sinuses were full of liquid he made very beautiful sounds. That is why I advised him to just think about his singing and not to confuse his sinus trouble with the resonators one uses for singing. So you see it is the whole body that vibrates.

CHAPTER 14

BREATHING

Mastery of the breath is fundamental to the acquisition of a good singing technique, but the entire art of singing cannot rest solely on breathing, any more than it can rest on the functioning of the tongue and pharynx, or on the larynx. Respiratory activity is one element of a complex structure that acts in synergy. Part of vocal training is learning to breathe so that the exhalation coordinates with the activity of the larynx. Once we acquire excellent listening, the mechanisms that regulate the larynx, pharynx, tongue, lips, etc., must be implemented and the vocal apparatus must function perfectly. When all that is mastered, singing indeed seems to be simply a matter of breathing.

Inhaling and Exhaling

The vital act of breathing, inhaling and exhaling, follows a rhythm that varies with age, activity, thoracic development, stress, and so on. It supplies air to the lungs where osmosis charges the red blood cells with oxygen and removes the carbon dioxide that results from cellular combustion by eliminating organic waste. The entire organism benefits enormously from our awareness of breathing. Many practices make use of complex respiration, notably yoga. Without going into these various techniques, we can say that they are similar to singing in that conscious breath control is required. How long it takes to acquire the kind of control you will need is an individual matter.

With breathing exercises as with exercises for the larynx, you will need patience. Acquiring exceptional mastery over the breath is a long and serious learning process. You need to acquire ample, calm breathing. Never work over tension or fatigue. Short sessions throughout the day will yield better results than one long session. Once the respiratory mechanism is well regulated, you have to integrate it with all the other proprioceptive sensations specific to singing.

Movement of the Diaphragm

In great singing, the most dynamic activity is carried out by the diaphragm. When expansion is maintained correctly, the vault of the diaphragm from its highest point at exhale will have an excursion of nine to eleven centimeters with a full breath. The clavicles are horizontal, the shoulders are relaxed back and wide, and the thorax is open with the ribs perpendicular to the spinal column (see fig. 14.1). It is as if you were lifting the rib cage sideways as though the ribs had hinges.

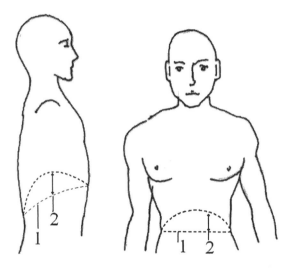

Figure 14.1 Diaphragmatic Movements of a Good Singer

1. Diaphragm. 2. Arrow indicates displacement of the dome of the diaphragm.

When the ribs are not raised at the sides, there are important consequences for singing. The excursion of the diaphragmatic dome is reduced to two or three centimeters, and the bottom ribs sink. The drooped position of the shoulders and clavicles do not permit diaphragm to spread out (see fig. 14.2). The entire posture suffers. The belly balloons out, and the pelvis is unsteady, undependable for support. The thorax will contract prematurely and prevent the diaphragm from functioning normally. With training, only the diaphragm takes part in respiration for singing. The thoracic muscles remain in relaxed extension so the ribs stay open and cannot exert too much pressure.

In fact it is not easy to consciously direct the movements of the diaphragm to retain the air and make it flow over the vocal cords without ever pushing. Inexperienced singers inflate the top of the thorax and leave the bottom part empty. Others do the opposite. In both cases this is a very fatiguing exercise that makes the instrument of singing a part of which is constituted by the thoracic cage, change shape constantly. This means that the sound is not always of good quality. Imagine if you were playing a violin and your violin kept changing shape as you played. You would be totally at sea. The thoracic cage must offer a volume and dynamic suitable for singing.

In order to avoid pushing when you sing, you need to notice certain proprioceptive sensations. When your body is free, these will change according to the register in which you are singing. The locations of these sensations move in the opposite direction from the sensation of pitch. The higher you sing the lower the sensation of support becomes. Do not confuse this with pushing down on the lower ribs, which will make you sing flat and goodbye career!

You feel low notes in the clavicles, at the top of the lungs. In the midrange, you feel the sternum. With high notes, the base of the thorax is engaged. Then, as you get nearer to the extreme high notes, you feel muscles in the lower abdomen engage. Since high notes are not used often, most of the time you will be working in the middle range, and you use only the excursion of the diaphragm. However, there is head tone in every note and that allows us to proceed from one register to another without audible gear changes.

The thorax, as expanded as possible and relatively immobile without being locked, assures phonation. Everyone has a different way of describing this. Gigli told me that he let his belly "fall to the ground" to breathe and maintained the same feeling as long as the breath stream lasted. That way the abdominal muscles do not interfere with the diaphragm. Some people teach singers to fill their lungs and then contract the abdomen to have "good support." This is wrong! Contracted abdominal muscles push the internal organs against the diaphragm, preventing its normal excursion. This is not proper support. Avoid it like the plague.

It is better to think of the rib cage as an enormous elastic container, mobilized at will. Some people compare it to a blacksmith's bellows or a chimney. Fill it until it is full. Empty it while closing the larynx a bit and voila: you're singing! If only it were that simple! This type of chest expansion has ruined many singers. Pressure tightens the larynx. The tenser the cords, the more you have to push, and then if you push harder, they get tighter still. The larynx suffers and the voice starts to wobble. The more proficient singers become in this technique, the more likely they are to damage the larynx. Anyway, when you do this, the thorax cannot vibrate, so there is no way for it to become a resonating chamber. When the singer allows the escape of the smallest amount of air possible, the larynx takes the following position and the thorax, already resonating, will expand more fully (see fig. 14.3).

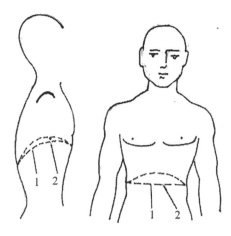

Figure 14.2 Diaphragm Movements of a Poor Singer

1. Diaphragm. 2. Arrow shows the displacement of the diaphragm. Note how slight this is.

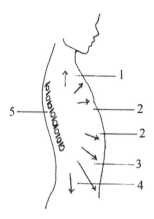

Figure 14.3 Proprioceptive Sensations of Support

1. High thoracic support. 2. Sternal support of medium pitches. 3. Low thoracic support of high notes. 4. Belly support for extreme highs (*sovracuti*). 5. Spinal column.

The Art of Breathing

Plato, and later Aristotle, said that in order to speak or sing well, one had to vibrate the whole body to bring the external air into unison with the air inside the body. That implies stillness in the breath. Indeed, breath control for singers calls upon special mechanisms. You must learn to conserve stored air and to give out the least possible amount, as if you were distilling the sonic flow in some way. You take in a comfortable amount of air, retain it and let it flow with absolutely minimal pressure. The more slowly and regularly the flow emerges, the less underlying tension results, and the more easily the larynx works. It freely adapts to the needs of the pharynx, which in turn adapts to the larynx. The pharyngeal-laryngeal acoustic circuit must be respected so that the larynx is free to modify on demand, as a function of tessitura, color, etc.

How do you go about closing the larynx as little as possible? How can you "not give" air? Certainly you need some flow of air to make sound. You have to use as slight an airflow as possible, and struggle against the reflex that will make you want to exert pressure with the thorax, and let all the air escape at once. When you are successful and the larynx vibrates this way, the cords are handled with great delicacy. Singers must be taught to act judiciously on the exhalation.

People speak of a column of air, a column of exhalation, etc. This is not a helpful image. Bear in mind we are speaking about several *grams* of air. Most singers, despite their best intentions, let too much air escape. When that happens, the result is a shout or what appears to be a controlled scream. Certain vocal techniques are based on thoracic pressure. Some use muscular effort located in the belly, others at the base of the back, at the edges of the thorax, sometimes even at the back of the ribs. Each technique is searching for the Holy Grail.

People who sing this way live so totally in their head, that they see what they are doing as logical and they can not feel what harm they are doing to themselves. For them the larynx is in fact like the mouthpiece of a wind instrument, which has to be pushed to make sound. That is absolutely wrong. But what is right?

The Column of Sound

What happens in normal respiration? In people who breathe without problems, the thorax enlarges slowly, increasing in volume beginning at the lower thorax and the gut, then at the base of the ribs and finally in the upper part, near the clavicles. The intake of breath is slow, relaxed, and spontaneous. At the apex of the inhalation, there is a pause for several milliseconds before a calm and unhurried exhalation begins. This action is global, as if the thorax were deflating. All the parts of the thorax yield slowly. When the exhalation is finished, there is a brief pause before the new inhalation. The thorax is an expandable vessel that fills and then empties, with pauses in between.

That being the case, what in the world makes singers tank up with air until we're ready to burst? It seems pretty clear that what motivates this "anti-singing," if there is such a thing, is the idea that sound is a dense discharge, like a jet of water that has to project over the greatest possible distance, as if we were watering a lawn. To do this you would need to have more air in your lungs than is humanly possible. So that's not it.

You have to take in a comfortable amount of air, no more. Then you distribute that air with minimum pressure, as if caressing the vocal cords. This excites the spinal column so that it too starts to sing. We want to make a column of sound, resonant over and under the glottis, not a column of air, as myth would have it.

The column of sound is superimposed on a column of breath. Without air, there is no sound. But it is one thing to talk about a column of air with all the ideas that are usually associated to it: the push, the pressure, tensions on the cords, etc., but a column of sound is something altogether different. The latter implies relaxation, a measured and tranquil expenditure, being on the lookout for tension, to reduce effort, to avoid pressure. The singer unblocks his thorax and experiences the joy of taking in just enough air and then distilling it and letting it flow on demand. His own experience of ample breath creates the same euphoria in the listener.

Singing well brings about the rediscovery of true respiration, calm and unstressed, with a natural physiological rhythm. The diaphragm is liberated, autonomous, not locked in expansion. You must be able to perceive this respiratory rhythm while singing, so that you can remember and analyze it outside of singing, as you go about your daily life.

Fashion has it that body volume and voice size are related, and that you have to develop muscles to acquire vocal intensity.

"She Lost her Voice Because She Lost Weight"

How many times have you heard that one? Many divas reach astonishing proportions, so people associate size with opera singers for good reason, without viewing it as a handicap. While it is understandable that singers should want to lose excess weight, it would certainly be a shame if the voice became smaller as a consequence.

There is hardly any correlation between vocal phenomenon and obesity, even if many singers are quite rotund. Losing weight does not make the voice smaller and weaker. You will often hear this when the voice goes as the singer becomes thinner. This is not true and I have the audiograms to prove it. If weight loss were to blame, the auditory system would have to deteriorate as weight normalizes. That is simply not the case. Weight loss does not harm hearing at all; in fact, it can help. So if obesity is not a necessary condition for singing, why are there so many fat singers?

Excess weight makes singers clumsy and awkward, restricting movement and vocal gesture. Above all, they suffer from respiratory difficulties. If they have difficulty breathing, how can they become experts in an activity that has inhaling and exhaling as its cornerstone? I believe it is precisely because they have so little energy that they become experts in singing. Their diminished strength is an asset. The great art consists of not pushing, of remaining in a state of supple tension, and of avoiding undue muscular effort.

It is difficult to achieve this lithe tension in some muscles while maintaining relaxation in the rest of the body. When the body is enveloped in fat, it becomes more and more difficult to tense your muscles, so attaining this elasticity obeys the law of minimum effort. It is harder to keep your muscles loose when you are thin and full of energy. So when a singer loses weight he will need to learn how to do this. It is almost like learning to breathe and sing all over again.

The Voices of Athletes

With young athletes, the more powerful their muscles, the more hoarse and more pushed their voices are. For a time, I followed two singers with muscles so developed they could have entered the Mister Universe contest. One, a Frenchman, was a champion body builder. He lifted heavy weights in the morning and again in the afternoon, accompanied no doubt by grunting sounds. You can imagine the muscles he had. How do you suppose he could avoid pushing? The smallest sound he made would have put tremendous pressure on his larynx. He asked me how he could learn to do nothing, when for him, doing nothing meant pressing twenty kilos.

The sounds that he made were neither beautiful nor big. They were devoid of resonance and so pushed and tense that he sounded as if he were strangling. In fact the vibrations were almost in inverse proportion to his physical strength. Our tenor was so powerful that he could never become any more than a bad student, no matter how hard he tried. He could not dose out the infinitesimal amount of air that he needed to satisfy his teachers; he was completely muscle bound.

The second singer was a prestigious American weight lifter. He had a huge thorax and enormous biceps, and everyone at the Paris Opera drooled over the thought of seeing him as Radames in *Aida*. He had the looks but the voice was so pushed that it was virtually nonexistent. All he could make was a choking sound with the ventricular bands, or false cords, which had enlarged to protect his cords from the damage that his underlying power would inflict during performance. My father was very strong as a young man, and even worked as a gym instructor for several years. He used to say that physical exercise hardens the voice, and this is most noticeable in the weight lifter. It might look great, but supple gesture becomes impossible, both for the body and for the vocal apparatus, which is essentially a group of muscles. (This is not an argument against being physically fit; it is a warning not to become muscle bound. Aerobics and moderate strength training are beneficial.)

Two more observations will illustrate the relationship between the voice and muscular strength. Many singers would come to my office during a long run of performances to complain that they were fatigued. Understandable! They would tell me that it was impossible to go on stage. After making sure they were in good vocal health, I would ask them to honor their contract. Each one would come afterwards to tell me he had never sung so well, that the voice had never been so flexible, so big, and so easy. Of course! They didn't push because they couldn't. Their general fatigue and muscular exhaustion would not permit it.

One particular singer allowed me to make an observation which I have since verified many times over in my work as voice specialist. When I was about sixteen, and still standing in the wings of the opera in Toulouse, I heard a newcomer. He was a Canadian light tenor who had come to the Capitol Theater to sing *Faust*. I remember his presence and the surprising clarity of his timber, an unaccustomed sound to the French ear. He had started with a career in operetta some years prior to his career in opera and comic opera.

His name was Raoul Jobin. His voice seemed a bit light for the Gounod at the time, but over the course of several years, he would establish himself in this role and go on to sing *Werther, Faust* and *Tosca.* Just as I was finishing my medical studies and establishing my career treating voices, he became a leading tenor at the Paris Opera, the tenor of choice in that repertoire. Ever more incredible, he took on heavier works: *Lohengrin, The Damnation of Faust* and then *Samson.*

Without ever dreaming of going beyond his first lighter roles, his voice acquired an enormously complex sound. As it grew, his high notes became even more brilliant. At the same time, he was progressively losing muscle from an athletic point of view. Though he never lost his strong stage presence, he had put on a bit of weight that gave him a riper kind of appeal, you might say.

As Jobin progressed in vocal size, he more easily mastered the control of his voice and his breathing. He was able to direct it with great flexibility and openness because he was no longer able to push. Singing is not an athletic activity: quite the contrary! Another example of ripeness of voice is Pavarotti's in his prime. Heaven knows his muscles are certainly well upholstered.

Many singers discover amazing facilities while pregnant, just as soon as their bellies start to swell. Although the popular belief is that this gives them especially good support, quite the opposite is true. Since they are unable to push with their abdominal muscles, the diaphragm is free to work by reflex action. A schematized circuit, auditory-brain-diaphragm, is at work, activated by the phrenic nerve. You can also think of it as the audio-cerebro-phrenic circuit. If these singers could remember how it felt to be free of muscular interference they could stay as free when the pregnancy is over. So what's the bottom line? You certainly don't have to be overweight to sing, but do be careful not to become overly muscular.

The Right Setting

Where is the middle ground? You do want to develop the musculature of containment, which will keep your ribs wide open, so your diaphragm is free to move spontaneously and automatically. Be aware of the muscles that permit the tongue to operate with just the minimal activity needed to articulate, without unnecessary constriction in the mouth, while the pharynx remains as open as possible.

Certainly all these movements and gestures are equally muscular. But they respond to a set of muscles that are the antagonistic push muscles, the flexors. Those that need to be exploited to the maximum are the extensors: the muscles that cause the body to be open, erect, vertical, with the thorax enlarged, etc. In becoming aware of this group of muscles, you can see how you might tend to overuse these antagonistic constrictor muscles until the flexors are sufficiently trained. You need a well-balanced synergy among them all. It is hard to open the pharynx, hold yourself straight, and breathe fully. But when you begin to associate all these movements, and get them to work simultaneously, singing suddenly becomes much easier.

Singing requires mastery over yourself to attain maximum acoustic sound output with minimum muscular effort. By doing as little as possible, a good singer lets his voice fly. His less talented neighbor will be shouting himself hoarse to produce a puny little sound. Can you see how much of vocal training turns out to be deconditioning? If you believe you have nailed singing technique immediately, it may be years before it dawns on you what this chapter is about. You will make better use of your time if you choose to speed up the process of gaining control over your listening and the reactions it regulates by taking advantage of modern electronic techniques.

Once you get the control, you keep working on it every day, with frequent repetitions at half voice, and only occasionally at full voice. The half voice is the test for vocal health and good singing. If you have no difficulty with half voice, rest assured you have a good technique. Very soon it will take on body and assurance as the whole body starts to resonate. It starts to vibrate quickly, adding undreamed-of amplification, resonating better and better. The architecture of the instrument changes, just as the body changes at the level of the skeleton.

As you keep singing, all the tensions that are normally present in a young and healthy body begin to diminish noticeably. You will get better results than are possible with any other school of technique. Breathing recovers its primary role in singing as the motor that sets the larynx in motion. Singing mobilizes the larynx with the delicacy of a virtuoso caressing his violin with the bow. The singer, now master of his breath, with his spinal column erect and comfortably seated over the sacrum, will have complete freedom of choice in his interpretation, as he breathes life into his vibrating, resonant body.

CHAPTER 15

VOWELS

Through a singer who was a close friend of Gigli, I was able to arrange a long meeting with this great artist. We met at his spacious apartment in the hotel George V in Paris, where he sat surrounded by a group of people that included his accompanist. He welcomed me warmly. After a few pleasantries, I began bombarding him with as many questions as I could think of.

How did he come to be a singer, how did he work, and so on. I was charmed by his passionate involvement in the subject and the rich detail of his answers.

When I asked the then sixty-one-year-old Gigli whether he still worked his voice, he said that he had worked on his vowels every day in front of a mirror ever since he had experienced vocal difficulties twenty years earlier. Although I was very excited by what Gigli was saying, I did not understand what he was talking about. However, after I told him about my experiments with audio-vocal reactions and how the ear modifies the voice, he responded by telling me in detail how he had recovered "his" vowels. Having chosen what he considered to be his best recordings, he listened to them with headphones while looking in a mirror. He reshaped his vowels by listening. The recordings that he used were "Cielo e mar" from *La Gioconda* and "M'appari" from *Martha*.

He said: "By training in this way, I realized that I had started to open my sounds too much; I was off the track. After realizing that, I was happy just to make the vowels shapes in front of a mirror without singing. I exercised by simulating each aria in this way, in vocal silence, strictly observing the shape and size of the vowel."

That gave me a lot to think about. I knew that he had touched on one of the fundamental issues of singing, but his explanation was incomplete. Perhaps Gigli could not give me any other details or perhaps I did not understand what he was telling me. I thought that this must be his gimmick. Many singers have special tricks that only work for them. Why not Gigli? Yet I sensed that it contained an essential key to vocal technique.

For years I had puzzled over the vowels because I knew that many singers, even professionals, found them difficult. They would tell me that they could exercise easily over a range of more than two octaves, but as soon as they had to add text to the musical phrase, the trouble would start.

In the work of Helmholtz on acoustics, he classified each vowel as belonging to a fixed note. So how could you even sing a score and follow the music if the vowels imposed their own physical presence in opposition to the words? This fundamental question of acoustics obsessed me for a long time.

What Helmholtz had stated was fleshed out in the work of Koenig, completed fifty years later. He too described the vowels as being from an "A" or a "B flat" going to an "A 1" for "an," "on" and "in," to "A 2" for "a," to the "A 3" for "o," to the "A 4"for "e" and D 6 for "i." It was fascinating to learn that volumes with well-defined colors are associated with each vowel. However this acoustic enigma, a curiosity in books, seemed to have no practical application. There appeared to be no practical application to singing, because not every F can be sung on an "A." How, for instance, would you sing "Celeste Aida" since the F is modified by the "a" B-flat?

For Gigli, what is more, the "I" vowels (pronounced in English ee) were the easiest to produce. Many singers have trouble with that vowel. He told me that the first thing he did with a new score was to underline all the "I" vowels because they served as resting places for him. It seemed that Gigli had his own special system for work. I kept mulling it over, knowing that some day a solution would come to me.

Engines that Can Sing the Vowels

While I was working on acoustic physiology at the Aeronautic Center in Chatillon-sous-Bagneux, my job was to assess auditory damage in employees working on jet engines at the Jet Propulsion Center at Saclay. In order to measure the effects, I needed to remove extraneous sounds, and isolate the noise produced by the engines. I used sonometers to determine sound thresholds, and spectrographic analyzers to decode the frequencies of each sound that I collected. I could determine the intensities of the sounds produced by these new engines and establish the intrinsic qualities of the various noises through a battery of tests. I also ran a study comparing auditory fatigue among the employees to find out if there was a correlation between the specific areas of the auditory test showing damage and the noises to which they had been subjected.

At the time the engineers were developing a new jet engine called the Atar, which later powered the Caravelle. The engine noise registered 130 decibels. One day, I went to the lab in Saclay. Thinking that the engine would not be tested that day, I did not take any equipment with me, but the engine was running. Opportunities to observe it at work were rare and there were few chances to take measurements. There would not be time to get my instruments before the engine was put to bed.

With assistance, I hastily put together some spheres of cardboard of various volumes. Since I knew the engine threshold was 130 decibels, I concentrated on frequencies in that spectrum. Thinking of the Helmholtz experiments, I wanted to catch the different frequencies of the noises made by the engine. I knew that when a sphere is subjected to a stationary wave containing a frequency that corresponds to its radius, the sphere resonates on the related frequency. This gave me a way to approximate some of the frequencies that started to ring in these balls. Only some frequencies could be measured, because I would have needed a larger number of balls to cover the whole range of frequencies. To detect the lows I would have needed larger balls than we could make with the materials we were using.

While I was in the process of making the various sizes of spheres and placing them around the huge engine, imagine my surprise when I heard each of them ring out one of the five pure vowels: a, e, i, o, u depending upon the size of the construction! I had just repeated the classic experiments of Helmholtz and Koenig. It was so exciting that I dropped everything else. I decided that the next time the engineers tested the Atar, I would concentrate on the vowels in order to determine what frequencies the engine was giving off. When I got back, the balls that I had carefully set side were as flat as pancakes. Clearly, someone in charge of cleanup had not realized what they were for. While I could never tease them back to their original round shape, I lucked out: they produced the vowels anyway!

I concluded that it has to be volume, not shape, that determines the effect. Here was the key to understanding what Gigli was saying about vowels in singing. Now I saw the connection between this experience and the experiment of Helmholtz and, later, Koenig. Gigli was right. Singing is essentially a business of making vowels. You must know how to focus them so they do not become a problem in singing. It comes down to the fact that there is one part of the body that sings if we allow it to, and another place where words are formed, and that the two had to be dealt with separately.

I needed to discover where vowels were formed and how they were fed. I knew I was onto something. Evidently, the volumes of the various vowels were seated in the mouth, but I still had to figure out how to form those cavities without interfering with the sound generated by the larynx.

Each vowel has its specific volume but not every volume makes a distinct vowel. All shapes make sounds, but a vowel has specific linguistic characteristics that distinguish it from all other sounds. The vowels sing with the voice and the sound they generate may take on additional coloration from the accompanying consonants.

In singing, we must distinguish between the cavity in which the vowels resonate, and the pharynx which itself resonates. The mouth cavity must remain autonomous to avoid hindering the other mechanisms of emission: bone conduction, breathing, or the adaptation of the pharynx and larynx. The movement of the tongue forms the cavities of the mouth.

With this in mind, we can now define the relative volume of each vowel. The demarcation line between the pharynx and the mouth is located in the place where you pronounce "g" as in the word go. (seefig.15.1). To do this, draw the lips gently forward. The point of the tongue rests gently against the inside of the lower teeth, right at the gum line. This is what we mean when we talk about forward pronunciation.

To sing without effort is one of the principal goals of the art of singing. If you should become fatigued, it means that there is some sort of problem that needs to be detected and eliminated. Any imbalance at this stage will lead to the pushing that results from a badly positioned separation at the back of the tongue. It can also cause improper vowel formation.

The volumes of the vowels are quite close to one another. The acoustic quality of each vowel is specific to its volume. Our job as singers is to make the distinctions between the vowels clear, and yet close to one another in their comparative volumes. The shape of the cavities is influenced by the anatomy of each singer.

Linguists describe the vowels in terms of the International Phonetic Alphabet (IPA). The use of the vowels in singing is a good deal simpler. We distinguish two groups of vowels: closed and open. No matter what language you are singing in, you use only the five pure Italian vowels. At the end of the sound, you "cheat" by coloring the sound with a last minute coloring of the vowel you need. The listener will perceive the vowel as having been the one they expect, but in practical terms, the prolongation of the sound you are making is a pure, easy Italian sound that will keep you free of tension.

In singing we need to reconcile these linguistic shapes so that they are as subtle as possible, and efficiently produced, so that we can pass from one to another with only the motion necessary for clear diction. Here as with the breathing, we pursue precision and minimal effort.

Note: The laws of physics and the limitations they place on vowel formation in singing has given rise to various strategies for creating clear pronunciation that is harmonious and beautiful throughout the registers. You can read about them in many books on vocal pedagogy, but what should be clear is that you will need a second pair of ears to guide you throughout your life as a singer.

The distinction between open and closed vowels is simply a way to compare two groups. When we talk about "closed mouth," the teeth still do not touch and the muscles in the lower jaw remain relaxed. No matter what the linguists tell us, we are not going to sacrifice free and easy production by overpronouncing the vowels. Clarity that is produced with tension will degenerate into muddy sound, so it serves no purpose to adhere to standards of pronunciation that are not congruent with good vocalism.

We say that open vowels require a slightly more open mouth, but it is more a matter of concept, since a slight separation between the tongue and the hard palate will always be present. It sounds rather more dramatic in the telling, than the subtle differences that characterize good enunciation. The tongue is often experienced as awkward at the moment of emission. To sing well you need to master the mechanics of the tongue in vocalization.

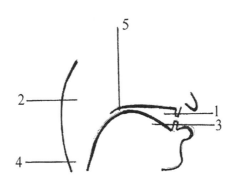

Figure 15 1 Phonating Posture

1. Anterior (oral) cavity. 2. Posterior (laryingo-
pharyngeal-nasal) cavity. 3. Tongue. 4. Larynx. 5. Area
where the "g" sound is produced.

The smile muscles at the corners of the lips do not pronounce the vowels so
reduce the activity of the risorius muscle to the absolute minimum. If you could
make a rectangle with your lips, then it is in the corners of that rectangle that the
lips lift up, stretch out, and extend, and not the real corners of the mouth. Working with the mirror as Gigli did will allow you to associate the shapes you are
making with the sounds you are producing.

This lip formation imparts a special tone to the muscles of the face, and, by
means of interacting with the facial muscles, to the muscles of the middle ear,
which give the ear optimal control over voice production. The cybernetic loops
between the muscles of the middle ear and the facial muscles are described in
Part II, chapter 4.

The pharynx resonance sets the resonance of the mouth in motion when there
is an agreement of impedance. You will have to learn to make minute adjustments in both cavities to create that agreement and assure a cleanly articulated
vowel. If you think about how many combinations are possible, you can see that
finding acoustic agreement between the anatomical cavities will take careful
attention. Once you find them you will need to make them yours.

How to Exercise to Form the Vowels

Each vowel has its own shape and volume. In all, about ten vowel shapes will
express any language in singing, five of them secondary. You will pronounce
the pure vowels and only add seasoning if necessary, just before moving on to

the next syllable. When you establish the mouth shape, the sound you make will be a complete and clear representation of that vowel.

Gigli's sensitivity led him to discover the optimal resonance cavity for each of the vowels while he was singing. He exploited his mouth conformation with great economy, giving him excellent sound and clear diction. This is an important accomplishment in singing. The better the pronunciation, the more easily the voice is placed and the better you sing, the easier it is to articulate.

Gigli said that he practiced his vowels daily in front of a mirror. Feeling, hearing, and looking at what you are doing at the same time gives you a clear sense of what you are doing. Even though you will notice a difference after only a few sessions, stick with it! It takes time to establish these habits permanently. By paying close attention to the vowels, you will obtain results more quickly. Anatomy makes the shaping of vowels a personal matter. You have to experiment to find your own clarity the same way Gigli found his. (Assuming that you already have mastered breathing and have a clear image of the vowels).

Think of the neuro-sensory-motor cavities of the mouth and pharynx as two separate spaces; the front one is the mouth; the posterior one is the pharynx. This latter cavity is wider and shaped like a funnel. It begins at the larynx and extends all the way to the nasal-pharynx. It is divided from the mouth cavity at the point where the tongue touches the palate.

When you can exploit this division you are ready to sing by putting the skeleton in resonance. Add the pharynx, naso-pharynx, and nasal annexes above it on one hand to the mouth. Vowels shaped in the mouth begin to sing spontaneously as soon as the bone and the pharynx are ignited by sound. In fact, the "vowel cavity" resonates solely in the presence of frequencies of sounds corresponding specifically to vowel formation.

Sounds produced by the larynx are controlled and fed by bone conduction; those coming from the pharynx travel over the same circuit to reach the inner ear. Sounds produced in the mouth, however, are fed by air conduction. Moreover, the vowel sound is perceived separately from the vocal timber. The more you respect the independence of these two phenomena, the more freely and easily you will sing, and the richer your voice will become.

Most awkwardness in singing develops when we add words. It is possible to vocalize from top to bottom but with words the issue becomes a great deal more complex. An incompatibility develops between sound and language when the cavities are incompletely separated. The resonance of mouth and pharynx are equally affected. The larynx loses its freedom and begins to compensate by closing. This causes pushing and the entire dynamics of singing disintegrates.

Even when the two cavities are separated vocal quality can still sometimes suffer. Any sort of effort to feed the mouth will distort the standing wave that he has set up in the mouth by creating the vowel shape. Helmholtz taught us that the resonator starts to sing through its proximity to the sound generator, in this case the larynx/pharynx. The singer must resist making any effort that might interfere with this acoustic phenomenon. The vowel will sing by itself once the singer has trained himself to stay out of its way. In singing, less is always more. Just find the exact shape of each vowel by regulating the mouth opening.

For example, let us suppose you have chosen the "a." If you start with the wrong volume, the vowel will be deformed; the voice will sound inharmonious. If you gradually increase the opening you will come to a point where the voice not only speaks more easily, but the sound will be ample and round. It is full, colored, and warm. What you are feeling is the acoustic pressure on the walls of the resonator; it causes a specific proprioceptive sensation, like having a soft apple in your mouth. If you continue to open beyond the point where the vowel becomes clear, it will start to lose brilliance, velvet, and ease. You will start pushing again and the vowel will lose precision because the shape is wrong.

Do the vowels remain identical on all pitches? Do you use the same resonating cavity in all the registers? In the low and medium registers, there is no change. The vowels remain the same from the medium high to the lowest notes. The pharynx, and even more so the larynx, adjust on their own as long as there is no interference from the vowels. (In female voices, diction is always less clear at F or above and the vowels have less definition.)

What happens in the high medium register? The opening changes very gradually as you climb. Does that mean that the volume of the vowel is not the same? Not at all. But a modification takes place, which upsets the previous structure and institutes a new one. The division between the pharynx and the mouth moves back. It follows the pharynx, which narrows a bit at the apex of its opening. This is not a constriction, but a smaller volume in the pharynx, which comes from a narrowing behind the tongue and at the sides of the pharynx behind the uvula as you rise in pitch.

This change in the pharyngeal canal to reach a higher tessitura is related to the structural modification or accommodation of the larynx-pharynx that takes place in the high medium register. The volume of the central cavity of the pharynx gets smaller. The tongue is, as a result, swept slightly backwards at the same time. The line of demarcation moves back accordingly. As a consequence, the mouth cavity has to change in order to maintain the same measurement. A few compensations are necessary: the mouth opens wider, the megaphone moves deeper, and the lips protrude less in the extreme high notes. You can still identify specific vowel shapes. In extremely high notes variations in volume between one vowel and another are so subtle that they may be more of an intention than a physical fact.

What really happens at the point of separation between the two resonating cavities? The tongue is often experienced as an important but bothersome element by singers. It is an important presence—how can one not feel it—but bothersome only because we do not know what to do with it. We know that it should not be contracted, but where do we put it? If it slides too far back, it reduces the pharynx.

If the position of the tongue is exaggerated, it will press on the larynx and spoil the sound. It cannot go too far forward, because the larynx will rise and if the tongue goes back, the larynx gets jammed down. Furthermore, the accommodations below the larynx and pharynx-mouth mean that the sound and the vowels are left more to chance. There are an infinite number of proprioceptive sensations that are difficult to integrate. Every note will have its own set of adaptations for each of the vowels.

Singing is within the reach of anyone who has good listening. If we accept that listening is essential, then singing is a normal physiological act which is easy to control and over which one can acquire mastery. The key to good pronunciation is the separation of the two functions. This separation makes it possible to combine two simultaneous activities, that of making vowels and that of the production of sound.

If the relationship between the tongue and the palate is wrong, it alters the arrangement of the pharynx-larynx. We know what happens then: pushing, closing, color changes, loss of facility, and the immediate loss of joy in singing. It becomes nothing but hard work.

You have to be continuously aware of the space through which the frequencies from the singing cavity (larynx-pharynx) spark resonance in the mouth. This tiny space between the palate and the tongue is only a few millimeters high. You will have to search slowly and patiently for the exact moment when the firing in the mouth takes place between mouth and pharynx.

In conclusion, the study of the vowels is the basis of fine singing for every voice, whatever the type of singing. Once you have acquired the basic vowels, let your teacher help you to discover the proprioceptive sensations associated with optimal use of the two resonators, mouth and pharynx. Once this practice becomes habit you will be able to turn your attention to interpretation. Habits are necessary for any kind of learning designed to create cybernetic circuits of control.

It is imperative for you to know the exact measure of your resonating cavities, to become conscious of their volumes, since they are linked to individual anatomy. There are as many vowel structures as there are anatomical conformations. As you have already learned, the volume for each vowel stays the same; only the shape changes. This shape determines the position of the lips, placing them more or less forward.

This is important. It is useless for a singer to waste time trying to imitate what another singer is doing with his face, no matter how great an artist he may be. His facial gesture belongs only to him. Imitate another singer only as a way to find the gesture specific to your own anatomy. Imitation can reveal the values of the vowels relative to one another since the size remains constant from one singer to another. The shape you need to make will vary; the volumes of all the vowels remain the same for everyone.

CHAPTER 16

FALSETTO

Falsetto is the term generally used to describe the unsupported breathy sound associated with an unbroken male voice. It is also used among voice teachers and cognoscenti to indicate the use of head voice both in male and female voices, and this is where the confusion begins. The true falsetto sound is easily recognized, as it is virtually impossible to dynamically alter it by crescendo or diminuendo without pushing violently with excessive breath or squeezing the throat muscles, resulting in an unpleasant hooting sound, devoid of all vibrato and resonance.

The current use of the word among singers and their teachers again varies from country to country. The Italian school uses its meaning correctly, substituting the words *falsettone* and *falsetto accomodato,* indicating that it is a supported sound principally of head resonance that will carry. Examples of this can be found in the many recordings of Beniamino Gigli among others, in his use of the piano and pianissimo passages of the songs and arias he sings. What is also plainly evident is that it is the core of the voice and any dynamic variant comes out of this basic sound, allowing crescendi and diminuendi with no audible gear change from register to register.

Men imitating women's voices in general use falsetto and with study can disguise the obvious limitations of this technique never, however achieving a true soprano or mezzo-soprano sound and remaining an oddity in the world of singing.

As you will read in the following passages, the use of the word falsetto has also been taken to mean covering.

Without the supported head tone described previously, passing from register to register becomes audibly jarring. Covering is the gradual altering of the shape of the pharyngeal cavity. With correct breath support and expansion of the ribcage, this allows the larynx to descend and the pharynx to expand accordingly. This will be a principal guide for the voice to rise in tone and brilliance, using more of the head voice and less of the chest register and achieving a seamless legato covering the vocal extension of the singer.

Clarification of the use of the word tessitura is essential. Tessitura is the term used to indicate the area of vocal range which becomes "home base" in a given aria, operatic role, or song. An example easy to understand would be: a tenor

singing a dramatic role such as Otello or Manrico would generally find the role
of Ernesto or Nemorino uncomfortably high, as most of the writing lies in the
upper part of the vocal range where more head voice is required without de-
scending for rest periods into the chest register. This does not mean that the
dramatic roles do not have high passages; they are generally few and for dramatic effect, whereas in the Bel Canto operas technical ability to sustain long
periods of singing in the higher part of the voice is essential.

Falsetto or covering is the structural preparation that ensures the passage
from chest voice to head voice. Each of the registers is differentiated by the
color of its timber. The place where we change from one register to the other is
known as the *passaggio*. Whether one sings in chest or head voice depends on
the tessitura.

The head voice should always contain elements of chest, and likewise the
chest voice is mixed with sounds in the head. It is considered by some that there
are three vocal registers: chest, middle, and head voice, while for others only
two—chest and head. It is also said by some that in men there are two overlap-
ping registers, while in women there are three distinct registers, that of the middle being called female falsetto. The fact of the matter is that these arguments
are based on proprioceptive sensations and are too subjective to prove.

The use of the chest register is certainly more predominant in the male
voice where it is used in at least two-thirds of the vocal extension. In women,
the reverse is true: where one-third of the vocal extension is in chest, two-thirds
in the head voice.

The passage from one register to the other must be made gracefully in order
to arrive at a homogeneous color. This can only be accomplished with careful
study and complete mastery of the correct method of breathing. Failure to master this element of the vocal technique will result in singers who sound as if they
have two or three voices.

In the breath support, there is a moment of relaxation that allows another
laryngeal-pharyngeal-pulmonary structure to take over. Whenever you change
speeds, you use the clutch: that is the falsetto. Just as the driver notices this shift
much more than the passengers, the audience will not detect jarringly sudden
shifts if the singer uses the falsetto well, to maintain total relaxation until the
moment when some new tension comes into play. If you follow this process into
the head voice, you may feel a second shift in the extreme highs, a new falsetto
if you like, the shift that allows you to reach another fifth higher (the *sovracuti*
or *in alt*).

Setting aside the *sovracuti*, for a moment let us go back to the first passaggio to falsetto. This extends over an octave. At any point along its extension,
you must be able to reengage and use full voice. As you exercise, you will notice that, at different points along the extension, the chest voice must be blended
progressively with head voice until finally you hear only pure head voice. The
falsetto allows you move into the head.

Shifting is a way of accommodating. This accommodation takes place both
on the way up and on the way down. Ideally the larynx operates with no tension

whatsoever, even on exhale. If you push, you cannot sing. In singing, exhaling is like swimming under water; you must dole out the air as slowly as possible. It is never about blowing off steam.

When you use falsetto to negotiate the *passaggio* it regains the pride of place it had in bel canto singing. This vital part of singing technique was nearly eclipsed by the pushed, gutsy sound that emerged with verismo. Taste dictated for a long time that this supposedly strong, courageous vocal utterance wore an air of almost moral superiority. The falsetto was considered for a time to be old fashioned and decadent. Those singers who continued to use it had to disguise it well. People had forgotten that the falsetto accommodato is the foundation of every sound we make. It is the only way to shift properly between registers. If you don't know how to make the necessary adjustments, you have a difficult approach to the high notes. The larynx does not move down freely and the voice becomes hard, straight, white, acid and lifeless. This is not bel canto, it is can belto!

This mechanism must be found in every voice from soprano to bass. Register changes always cause a modification of the laryngeal-pharyngeal respiratory structure. You do not have to be able to recite the anatomy of all the ligaments and muscles involved, but you do have to know their location as precisely as possible. The feeling of relaxation is so clear that once you get it, it is easy to make it a habit, so that you can go in and out of chest and head at will. You will have to be patient and persistent to learn to do this so gradually and elegantly that the shifts become imperceptible to the listener.

Negotiating the *passaggio* is the acid test of a good vocal technique. If you don't get the hang of it, your vocal cords have to withstand inordinate punishment, and you will never be able to make the necessary shifts. There is nothing artificial about falsetto; it is a mark of good technique. You have never really sung at all until you have experienced the beautiful *mezzavoce* sounds that become available to you with falsetto.

The kind of color you get from using a mix of falsetto is absolutely gorgeous. When you do your preparation for singing, you use falsetto. It is the basis for every sound you make, so use it for study and gradually mix in more intensity and volume where you need it, while always conserving your connection to this underlying quality. Every attack starts gently, with the kernel of the pitch. This is the way the voice works. Always go from soft to full voice, rather than starting with singing full out and then trying to tone it down. It doesn't work.

Gigli and the *Falsetto Accomodato*

Gigli told me the secret of his high notes—the highest fifth. It was the *falsetto accomodato*. However, he asked me never to speak of it during his lifetime and I have respected his wishes. You can imagine what an uproar it would have created while he was alive. People would have called him a wimp and a phony. At that time verismo was at the height of its fashion. The falsetto was an absolute no-no, especially in Italy. Beniamino Gigli wanted us to know that the head voice takes on a special coloration in this resonance when the *accomodato* is introduced. First we need to understand what he meant by the term *accomodato*.

It is true that pure falsetto produces a flat, empty sound without density. The sudden relaxation of the larynx allows a totally different adaptation of the structure of the vocal cords. It is easy to find. A different sensation announces the modification. There is a physical shift, when you pass a certain pitch height. However, when you go high enough, this sound suddenly takes on body, responding to laryngeal tension different from that of the other registers. Using posture and facial mobility for the closing of the nose and of the movements of the soft palate, the sound takes on the color needed for the high notes. The *accomodato* responds to this secondary preparation. In reality, it is the only way to get to the extreme high notes easily with good color and quality. But we are not supposed to say so. With his consummate artistry, Gigli had perceived the essential difference between the registers caused by this anatomical shift that takes place in the larynx. Without this subtle mechanism, you will end up pushing and the sounds will be forced, tight, and very dangerous to the larynx.

Young singers have to get control over this mechanism. It is the only way to sing easily and create ethereal, mysterious, dense, vibrant, clear, warm, clarion sounds that mark the great singers. This is what the old masters preached; in order to have a relaxed larynx you have to relax your body completely—you must do nothing! Then it begins to vibrate as if by magic, without expending any energy at all.

It takes some work to get the feeling of ascending the scale without expending any energy at all. You have to learn to differentiate between the kind of energy that seems necessary to rise in pitch, and tension in the larynx. It is easy to confuse going up in pitch, with its attendant naturally increasing intensity, with the need to employ effort, which is entirely unrelated. The intensity of the sound comes from avoiding any pushing, so that the larynx is free to drop slightly lower. As we have already discussed, the sensation of support will shift lower in the body at the same time.

It might seem to people as if you have to push more air to go up in pitch; the higher you go, the more careful you have to be not to allow any pressure to intrude. I have already talked about this in connection with breathing and with the larynx. Pitch height and effort can seem to be in direct relationship but in fact the two factors operate in inverse proportion.

For now, remember that the larynx has to feel as if it had suddenly relaxed. Tension underneath the larynx is virtually nonexistent, not at all like the kind of force some singers use when they try to hit a high note. Falsetto only operates with the lighter mechanism of the head voice. It is not as useful, and does not really start to work, until you get to the highest position, the last shift that the larynx makes. There is an entirely different kind of tension, and you will realize how to use it.

From one register to the other, from one *passaggio* to the other, the larynx accommodates to its new emission according to pitch. This is not a gradual modification. It is a succession of dynamic modifications of the laryngeal structure associated with a complex interplay of pharynx, rhino-pharynx, mouth, and of the manner of breathing. Every time you pass from one register to another, the larynx has to physically shift and settle into its new alignment. The actual mechanical change is sudden. It involves shifts in the larynx, pharynx, the part of the pharynx that includes the nose (nasopharynx), the mouth, and the way the breath is used. The professional singer must learn to disguise these changes. That is the whole art of negotiating the *passaggio*. The notion is very important.

Think of the top fifth as an accommodation of an accommodation. The falsetto is already a special way to use the voice. This action entirely modifies the activity of the vocal apparatus. If falsetto is really is a "clutch" how do we make it into a legitimate element of the voice? To adjust sound in the *passaggi* we have to let the shift happen. The larynx, pharynx, and breath assume a new relationship. Then you have to add the nasal action. This is essential.

Now it is time to consider the role of the nose. Whenever we talk about the pharynx making sound, there is always some activity in the nostrils. In the low and medium registers it is a cavity that oita at the top of the pharynx. Once you get to the *passaggio* and above, it helps to create a new structural alignment in the larynx and the pharynx. If you want to keep using a light sound the nasal passages act the same as in the falsetto. The minute you want to add body to this characteristically weak sound, you have to close the nasal passages by flaring out the muscles at the wings of the nose. The muscle that raises the upper lip works in conjunction with this pair of muscles, so you flare out the nostrils and raise the upper lip into a slight smile. Make sure the muscles at the corner of the mouth do not come into play.

In Gigli's day, all that nonsense about dragging the chest register into the head (*di petto*) was in fashion. If anyone had heard him say anything about the falsetto, he would have discredited himself with the screamers who were all the rage in verismo. So rather than start a controversy, he kept his technical strategies to himself. But he wanted to make sure to pass the torch to future generations. So he confided his use of the falsetto to me as if it were a military secret, to be released after he was gone, so that nobody would be able to use this information to harm his career. The "new thought" had destroyed vocal progress for nearly a hundred years since the advent of verismo, misleading everyone and nearly destroying the art of bel canto.

Does this "new" way of singing require a refined vocal technique? I should say not. It is all about yelling. It is natural to sing but people can be very clever at finding ways to fiddle with things that need to be left alone. It is all too easy to intellectualize and mess with Mother Nature. The education we receive too often runs counter to spontaneous learning.

Singing is innate. All its mechanisms are automatic. Yet, they depend on a profound neurophysiologic structure, which can be deranged by bad usage. It is appalling to see the aberrant ideas that masquerade as vocal technique. Basically, the art of singing consists mostly in rediscovering our natural abilities. Some people have the good fortune to remain vocally intact, and all they have to do is become consciously aware of what they are already doing. They will of course have to fine-tune their coordination. Through the help of science they can speed up the process and get control of all the mechanisms that make up the neurophysiologic structure that is singing.

Finely schooled singing utilizes what occurs naturally and rejects artificial effects. We learn to play with virtuosity on all the mechanisms and the synergies of movement that are already there. This is what we call bel canto. Singing is a natural act, easy to exploit when it has not been altered, easy to find again if it goes off track. Pathological cases in which the ability to sing has been permanently damaged are the exception.

To recap, in accordance with what Gigli said, singing rests on the falsetto. You can't try to eliminate it. Quite the contrary; it must be exploited in the range where it exists. This is the right way to sing because it responds to the organization inherent in the larynx and pharynx in relation to frequency. Singers, you must use the falsetto; experiment with the mechanisms, and use them deliberately. Exploit them as fully as you can.

CHAPTER 17

WHAT IS NEEDED TO SING WELL?

This is the most important question for every singer, whether amateur or professional. All the mechanisms that have been described illuminate the capital role of the ear. We know that body posture, as well as posture for singing, depend entirely on the ear, so first of all you need to check your hearing, to be sure that your ear is in condition for you to be able to listen to yourself. Then, and only then, can you mobilize all the aptitudes necessary for singing to reach its optimal proficiency.

When the ear is ready, automatic responses activate, drawing on the innate ability to listen, which engages people to sing and speak. Both singing and speaking require a posture, which allows the vestibulocochlear system to position itself so that the neuromuscular and sensory responses facilitate emission.

There are no miracles. Even if you are gifted with a natural voice, you will need a wise and accomplished master to listen to you, one who knows how to conserve your initial resources and enhance their effectiveness. Electronics makes it easy to awaken sensations that are difficult to explain to beginners, and guard against unnecessary risks to the instrument during the beginning phase of study.

With a neurophysiologic foundation solidly established, the singing teacher will have a student who is ready to listen to him and profit from his teaching. There will then be no difficulties arising from the distortion of a badly prepared ear. Both student and master benefit. What the teacher says will resonate in the student who will correctly interpret what is required as training progresses. They will speak the same language and perceive things in the same way.

Evaluation of Listening

How do we know that the student has a good ear? We begin by evaluating the person's ability to listen:

- The potential of a person to differentiate and analyze frequency sequences.

- Whether the person has integrated the notions of space and time in the perception of sounds. In another words, does he know where a sound is coming from? Can he discern a sequence of pitches?
- Whether the person has good pitch discrimination, and
- Whether ear dominance has been established.

Auditory laterality is a very important since only the right ear regulates audio-vocal activity. Right ear dominance is one of the characteristics of a musical ear. If it is not fully present, it can be achieved through training.

The Musical Ear

Figure 17.1 represents the profile of a musical ear. It indicates a person who loves music, has good pitch control when he sings, and possesses a warm timber and rich color. It should come as no surprise that the profile of good hearing is the profile of the musical ear. It produces a graph similar to the one below for pitch height and intensity.

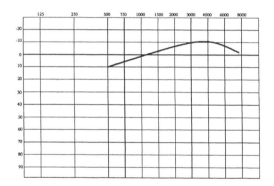

Figure 17.1

The frequency spectrum shown on the graph goes from lows at the left to the highs at the right. The volume threshold is measured in decibels. This diagram reflects ideal hearing in an ear without problems. Under normal conditions and from a physiological point of view, it is possible for anyone with normal hearing to acquire such a profile. Teaching a student with such a profile is easy. However, organic or psychological causes can also modify the shape of the curve, and then profound impacts can manifest in several ways:

- The body dynamic is modified by the action of the vestibule and
- The frequency analysis can be disturbed and more or less sensed by the cochlea.

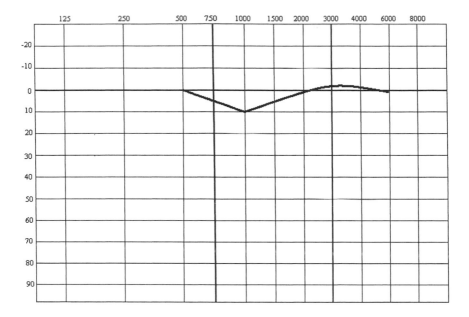

Figure 17.2

The profiles of the thresholds suggest different response patterns to sound. Some are particularly significant. For instance, if the diagram shows a dip between 500 Hz and 1000 Hz, the person is insensitive to music (see fig. 17.2). If the variation in the curve occurs between 1000 Hz and 2000 Hz, pitch is faulty (see fig. 17.3).

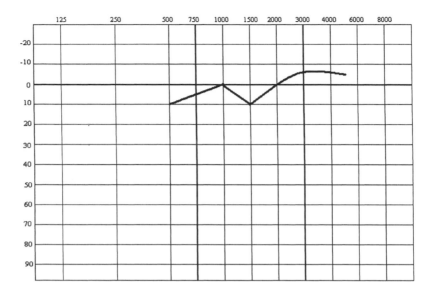

Figure 17.3

If the curve is inharmonious above 2000 Hz (see fig. 17.4), the quality of the voice is damaged, especially in timber and color.

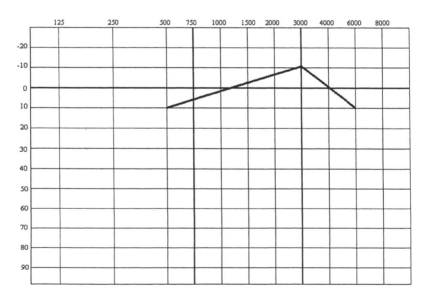

Figure 17.4

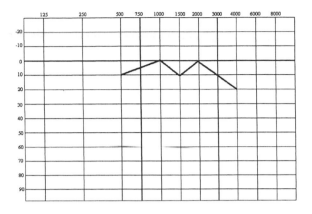

Figure 17.5

If the curve is still ascending from 500 Hz to 1000 Hz, but is strongly disarticulated above 1000 Hz, (see fig. 17.5) in the direction of the high notes, an affinity for music exists without the possibility of reproducing it.

Note: Absolute pitch is the ability to name each note of the scale. This is not necessarily a musical ear. It is possible to be able to identify every note and still not be musical. I knew a man at the Arsenal who had an absolute ear all the way to 2700 Hz. The normal ear goes to 1600 Hz. He was not in the least musical. What is important for the musician is relative pitch, the ability to identify intervals and harmonies.

Finally, if the curve is disarticulated (figure 17.6) or if it is flat (figure 17.7), neither musicality nor the possibility to reproduce musical sounds exist.

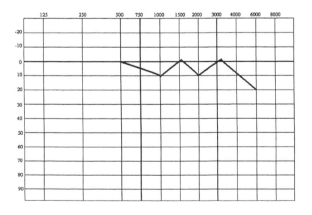

Figure 17.6

Under optimal conditions for musicality, (a talent for making or appreciat-
ing music) the quality of the voice is strongly influenced by the anatomy of the
speech apparatus specific to each individual. Musicality depends on the whole
neurophysiologic structure. It is universally true that the voice reflects a state of
mind. This is of course true for the musician. We assume he will have the ability
to execute the score precisely in tune, and he will still have to make other adjustments that depend on his mental state as well as his technique and the quality
of his instrument.

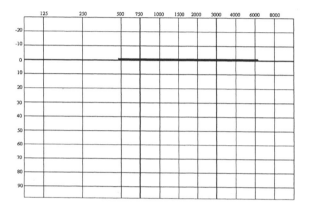

Figure 17.7

I had to reeducate a monk some time ago who had given up an international
music career. He was considered a great pianist and because of that, when he
entered the monastery they put him in charge of the choir. He felt uneasy because he had a great deal of difficulty with intonation and memorization in singing. As I knew the abbot, he sent the monk to me so that I could adjust his ear.

As a young man he had become famous as a great pianist through sheer effort. His mother was determined that he pursue music, so she put her son in the
hands of the great pianist Cortot. Day and night, the poor child played the piano.
He finally became a musician because of his great intelligence, but not because
of his sensibilities. That said, he had suffered all his life, and ended up running
away to a monastery. I hope he had some reason other than those I put forth because you can imagine he had problems with his musicality from the start.

He had only learned his music through his eyes and his hands, not with his
ears. That is true of certain pianists. I have met quite a few who were not musicians. Their listening tests show an important lack of musicality, and then of
course their instrument is already tuned for them. In fact a good many pianists
use only their eyes. A true musician is one who can hear a score and then play it
by ear. One pianist who was especially visual turned the pages as he played even

when he didn't have a score in front of him. He had attained a certain conditioning that made him a piano mechanic.

After training with the Electronic Ear, our pianist turned monk began to discover that he loved music and he could sing. This was an extraordinary revelation for him. Now he is the conductor of the choir of his monastery without any problem whatsoever.

Evaluation of Audio-Vocal Control

Once we know that hearing is satisfactory and open to listening, it is time to make sure that the audio-phonic regulatory circuits are well established. Singing not only depends on the ability to listen to oneself sing, it implies an assemblage of controls that are extremely elaborate and can fortunately be made automatic through continuous practice. The act of singing calls for a high level of cerebral control.

Psycho-sensory education can facilitate the process of learning to make music. (Although it is not strictly part of our discussion, it is important to note that it will also facilitate artistic and creative activity in actors, dancers, writers, and painters, to name a few of the other applications.) Even when hearing is good and listening begins to develop, it can still take quite a long time to master audio-vocal controls. Fortunately, auditory training shortens the time it takes to awaken and excite the whole sensory-motor system and cuts down the time needed to master a complete vocal technique.

Sometimes trouble of one sort or another can make it necessary to reconstruct control circuits in an experienced singer, whether damage is caused by intense professional activity, stress, faulty technique, or health issues.

The Electronic Ear

A listening device is used to establish the kind of audio-phonic reactions that lead to good singing. The training takes place through two channels: bone conduction and air conduction.

Sounds are fed through special headphones to the ears (air conduction) and to the top of the skull with a small vibrator (bone conduction). The key element is the fact that the sound is delivered through bone and air reception.

An electronic gating system alters the sound and exercises the muscles of the ear rather like priming a pump, revitalizing the automatic mechanisms which allow the middle ear to experience the ideal listening curve. The gating systems operate through bone conduction by exercising the muscle of the stirrup which regulates pressures within the inner ear, and through air conduction by exercising the muscle of the hammer which regulates the tensions of the tympanic membrane.

A specific program is designed, which in most cases allows the ear to regain a desirable profile and establishes a lasting ability to listen, with enough sessions to make the training permanent. However, this program is only useful for correcting alterations in function caused by poor education or psychological problems. It does not effect conditions stemming from organic causes such as nerve damage. The training is of short duration. There are fifteen days of training sessions, usually followed by a pause and one or two other shorter blocks of training.

In a couple of months the audio-vocal controls are in place, making the ear sensitive to its new aptitudes. At the same time, the neuro-sensory-motor areas that will be used for singing are now mobilized. Integration takes place gradually after training, and continues without further listening being necessary.

Note: Training over time is necessary for permanent results, and the length of training can vary from individual to individual.

What happens to those with decidedly poor listening? Their potential can be noticeably improved. The initial listening assay will indicate what needs to be addressed in order to achieve excellence in listening. With bad hearing, however, the situation is more complex. Some people can recover while others will see some measure of improvement. People with severely damaged ears rarely feel like singing.

Once the ear knows how to listen, the singer is able to analyze and memorize his own proprioceptive sensations with greater ease and speed. His singing becomes richer and stronger as he gains mastery over his listening and voice. With auditory education, it is possible to more quickly acquire the proprioceptive sensation indispensable to singing. When it is functioning at peak, after some years of training, the left ear will learn to process at the same speed as the right, bringing you to an elevated level of consciousness that is the hallmark of virtuosity, in other words of exceptional listening.

Audio-Vocal Training

Generally, after the first fifteen days, singers will usually be ready to benefit from some hands-on audio-vocal work to bring the auditory training that has been received to a conscious level. Singers will then be able to reproduce what they have learned by themselves. Not only will they listen, they will also learn how to listen to themselves. After mastering all the following circuits, they will become more sharply aware of their own instrument as they sing.

- The ear-larynx circuit,
- The ear-pharynx circuit,
- The ear-mouth circuit (vowels),
- The ear-lung circuit, and
- The ear-posture circuit.

Audio-vocal training first covers the listening posture and the singing posture to awaken awareness of the various parts of the body. The next objective is

CHAPTER 18

CONCLUSION

Allow me to conclude by extending my warmest invitation to each of you, to sing. If I have persuaded you to do this, if I have awakened a desire in you to make singing part of your life, then I have achieved my goal. If you seek every opportunity to revel in the joy of making music, I will be fulfilled. The most essential benefit for you is indisputably its potential to energize the brain with the stimulation triggered by singing. You will experience a greater sense of well being, enhanced vigilance, and improved body posture. At the same time, you will reach a higher level of consciousness and you will notice that you are more alert and engaged. There is simply nothing as good as the sound of your own voice when it is well used for charging the brain.

Of course, there are other ways to obtain this energizing effect. For example, musicians when they play are bathed in this universe of sounds, as are music lovers who seek opportunities to surround themselves with music and song. But the sound that we make ourselves, even if it is only humming, has a higher value for the brain.

You can see now that such an exercise is useful and that the capacity to sing is inherent in every one of us. I hope you will make it part of your life. You need not be a professional to enjoy singing, any more than you have to be a graphic artist to have fun drawing and painting.

Singing is one of the most complete means of expression available to us. It takes you on a journey of self-discovery and will help you develop a sense of yourself just as dance or sports do, yet, in a more complex and profound way. Your sensations will not be confined to the organs involved in singing. It sends acoustic stimulation to every part of the body, encouraging it to adopt certain postures. It helps to straighten the trunk, for instance, which helps it resist the pull of gravity, thus increasing the charging effect on the brain. When singing is well executed it triggers a wealth of internal sensations that make the body into a vibrating instrument.

This book emphasizes the role of the ear in singing, because those who want to sing, those who teach, and those who sing professionally generally take the role of the ear too much for granted. It is of paramount importance to take good care of your ears: they are fabulous but fragile organs. When you shampoo your hair be sure to rinse all the soap out or your ears will start to produce excessive wax to protect themselves from the chemicals in the soap.

A singer must exercise real discipline in taking care of his ears. He must avoid certain activities, like shooting or diving that are dangerous to his hearing. He also must avoid places that are excessively noisy. He should mistrust equipment, such as headphones of poor quality that can damage his hearing, and must eliminate medications that are dangerous to the ears. If you get sick you should be moderate in your use of antibiotics. You are no doubt aware that streptomycin and kanamycin can make a person deaf forever. You should always remember that cortisone can make you feel very cheery but if your vocal apparatus is suffering because of bad technique, cortisone will only mask the problem. Cortisone also has many long-lasting side effects that can be a significant detriment to your health. It is to be handled with kid gloves.

When loud environments like planes and subways are unavoidable, singers can benefit from using clean earplugs. It is never a good idea to study music in a noisy environment, nor to listen under those circumstances. We are not aware of how loudly we would have to adjust volume to make something heard over the noise of an engine. It is a better idea to leave study for another time. The noise itself causes fatigue and earplugs or noise canceling headphones can help you arrive at your destination in better shape. You need to avoid all sounds that discharge your energy. Generally these will be lowered sounds, free of high harmonics, such as drumbeats.

Singers must follow a diet based on food that tends to avoid a buildup of mucus that could cause trouble in the ears, nose, and throat. Everyone is different of course, but it is sensible to avoid foods that produce too much acid. Likely candidates are nuts, dairy products, sugar and starch, alcohol and meat.

The deafness of Beethoven was partly tied to what he ate. He was very fond of aged game, even though his friends refused to eat at his house because it smelled so bad. They spent their time at the window while Beethoven ate his spoiled meat. He wrote a great many letters in which he linked his deafness to the state of his intestines. He often wrote to his doctor and he used to tell him, "I can hear better because my intestines are better" or the reverse "It is a catastrophe. I can't hear a thing, my intestines are not working and my liver doesn't work."

We all need to stay well hydrated—singers more than most. You will only sing at your best if you are in good health and get plenty of rest, eight hours of sleep—for most of us. Professionals gladly observe these precautions because they are accustomed to protecting their vocal apparatus.

They should also have their hearing and listening checked every two or three years to find out how they are doing, and plan on a short course of listening to refresh their ears every so often. Listening is a good idea for anyone who wants to sing or to join a choral group, or before starting lessons.

While these are only suggestions, it seems to me that as soon as anyone is made aware of the possibilities for enhancing study and performance, they may be curious to try listening. It may just be a question of time before we see a wider acceptance of these strategies.

Fifty years ago, merely proposing these ideas was scandalous. Now consciousness has been raised. It takes about forty years for a new idea to be adopted. The first twenty years are the developmental stage when the ideas are known only to a small number of people, and another twenty years to bring the ideas to a wider public, as more discoveries support them.

Remember: *we sing with our ear.*

SELECTED BIBLIOGRAPHY

Bellis, Terry James. *When The Brain Can't Hear*. New York: Pocket Books, 2002.

Castro, Anthony. *Neuroscience: An Outline Approach*. St. Louis: Osby, Elsevier Science, 2002.

Clark, John L. E. editor. *A Visual Guide To The Human Body*. New York: Barnes & Noble Books, 1999.

Clemente, Anthony. *Anatomy*. 4th Edition. Baltimore: William & Wilkins, 1997.

D'Angelo, James. *Healing With The Voice*. Hammersmith, London: Thorsons, 2000.

Eliot, Lise. *What's Going On In There*? New York: Bantam, 1999.

Goldstein, E. Bruce. *Sensation And Perception*. Pacific Grove, CA: Brooks/ Cole Publishing Company, 1989.

Haines, Duane. *Neuroanatomy: An Atlas of Structures, and Systems*. Baltimore: Lippincott, William and Wilkins, 2000.

Larsen, William J. *Anatomy: Development, Function, Clinical Correlations*. Philadelphia: Saunders, Elsevier Science, 2002.

Leeds, Joshua. *The Power Of Sound*. Rochester, VT: Healing Arts Press 2001.

Netter, Frank. *Atlas Of Human Anatomy*. East Hanover, NJ: Novartis, 1989.

Madaule, Paul. *When Listening Comes Alive*. Ontario: Moulin Pub., 1993.

Restak, Richard. *Mozart's Brain And The Fighter Pilot*. NY: Three Rivers press, 2001

———. *Brainscapes*. New York: Hyperion.1995.

———. *The New Brain (How The Modern Age Is Rewiring Your Mind)*. Rodale, 2003.

Seashore, Carl. *Psychology of Music*. New York: Dover, 1938.

———. *The Secret Life Of The Brain*. Washington, DC: Joseph Henry Press, 2001.

Tomatis, Alfred. *The Conscious Ear*. NY: Station Hill Press Inc., 1991.

———. *The Ear And Language*. Ontario: Moulin, 1996.

Twietmeyer, J. Alan, and Thomas McCracken. *Coloring Guide To Human Anatomy*. Philadelphia: Lippincott, William and Wilkins, 2001.

Wilson-Pauwels, Linda, Elizabeth Akerson, and Patricia Stewart. *Cranial Nerves: Anatomy and Clinical Comments*. Hamilton, Ontario: B.C. Decker, Inc., 1988.

Index

accurate pitch distinction, 3, 12–13,
21–24, 32, 51, 79, 84, 98, 122, 125
acoustics, ix, x, 7–14.
See Helmholtz; Saclay vowel experiment
attention, 26, 43
auditory control loops. *See* control
loops
audio-vocal, xiii, 10, 13–15, 18, 32,
72, 76, 84, 86, 107, 122, 127–28
auditory fatigue, x, 22–23, 108
auditory fatigue test. *See* Peyser
auditory reeducation, 14, 34

Benedictines, 9, 10
bone conduction, x, xiii, 43, 66–67, 72,
91, 93–95, 96, 109, 129
breath control, 74, 97, 101
breathing, x, 12, 18, 21, 26, 32, 39, 71,
87, 89, 97, 101, 103–105, 109,
112, 116, 119, 129
diaphragm, 62, 74, 89, 98–105
pushing, 3, 99, 103, 110, 112–18
support, 18, 21, 24, 30, 80, 98–
104, 115–16

Campagnola, 8, 27, 28, 31
Caruso, Enrico, x, 8, 15, 27–31, 91
coach-accompanist, 80
column of sound, 101–102
control loops, 67
cortical charge, 9
cortical recharge, 5
cybernetic circuits. *See* feedback loops

deafness, professional, 12, 29, 80, 134
Dens, Michel, 23
diction, 110, 112–13, 130

ear, anatomy, 46–60

cochlea, 22, 45–58, 66, 83–85, 89,
91, 95, 122
external ear. *See* ear, anatomy
hair cells, 45, 51, 84, 86
hammer, x, 48–53, 59–60, 70, 86,
127
inner ear, 14–15, 32, 45–57, 59,
67, 74, 85–86, 112, 127, 129
labyrinth, 15, 45–49, 51, 85, 90
middle ear, 32, 48–52, 55, 59–61,
86–87, 111, 127, 129
saccule, 47, 51, 55, 83
stirrup, x, 32, 48–50, 52–53, 59–
62, 68, 70, 86, 127
semi-circular canal, 83
utricle, 47, 51, 55, 83, 86
vestibule, 38, 46–47, 52, 55–58,
66, 76, 83–86, 89, 95, 122
ear, damaged, 12, 128
ear, electronic, x, 8–9, 14, 18, 28, 74,
105, 127,130–31
ear, embryo, 59, 61, 83–84
ear, musical, 122, 125, 129
ear, right, x, 10, 14–15, 21–28, 33, 72,
76, 81, 87–92, 122
exercises. *See* vowel formation;
listening posture
extension, vocal, 115–16

facelift, 32
facial muscles, 32, 60, 68, 74, 87, 111
falsetto, 115–20
falsetto accomodato, 115–18
fatigue. *See* auditory fatigue
feedback loops, 58
filters, 14–15, 74, 91–92
Forti, Victor, 19
Francescati, Zino, 24–25, 130
Froeschels, doctor, 3

Gigli, Beniamino, 24, 27, 31, 99, 107–
    120.
    See also falsetto; falsetto accomo-
    dato; vowels

Helmholtz, 108
hoarseness, 32

integrators, xiii, 25, 57, 85

labyrinth. *See* ear, anatomy
larynx, 3–4, 9, 11–12, 28, 30–35, 39,
    44, 61, 63, 66–67, 70–76, 80, 89–
    95, 97, 99 101, 105, 109, 111–20,
    128–29
    nodules, 33–35
listening:
    inner voice, 43
    listening curves, 16, 32, 94, 130
    self listening, 8, 34, 43.
    See bone conduction; accurate
    pitch control or distinction
listening posture, 9–10, 26–27, 52–54,
    85–88, 91–93, 134–35

mechanisms of singing, 22, 26
memory, memorization, 84, 129, 131
metaphor in teaching voice, 81, 93
microphone, 13–14, 23–24
mind-body integration, 26
muscles of mastication, 59–61, 74

Peyser, 23
phonograms, 28–30
pitch and pitch problems. *See* accurate
    pitch distinction
plastic surgery. *See* facelift
posture:
    phonating, 111
    listening, singing, 9, 66, 68, 81,
    83, 85–86, 93, 95, 128
proprioception, 27
    proprioceptive sensations, xiii,
    17–18, 39, 84, 93, 97, 99–100,
    113–16, 128

reeducation, 8, 14, 28, 32, 35
right ear. *See* ear
    right voice, 75
Saclay vowel experiment, ix, 108

support. *See* breathing

teacher, voice, 95, 118

vagus nerve, 61–63
vocal cords, 3–4, 12, 14, 18, 32–33, 71,
    76, 90, 99, 101–103, 117–18
voices, 27, 30, 43, 80, 92, 95
    of athletes, 103, 112, 115–16
    left voice, 25, 75
voice teachers. *See* teacher, voice
vowels. *See* Gigli, Beniamino
vowel formation, 110, 112

weight loss, 102

ABOUT THE AUTHORS

Alfred A. Tomatis, (Nice, January 1, 1920 – Carcassone, December 25, 2001) received his M.D. from the Faculte de Paris before specializing in ear, nose and throat, and speech therapy. His first work with singers as house doctor at the Paris opera led to his subsequent discoveries. He was the first to describe the bones of the inner ear as functioning to protect against loud noises. He described the feedback loop that links the ear with the voice, which became his first law: the voice can only reproduce what the ear can distinguish. His discovery was made official by the Academy of Science and Medicine in Paris in 1957 and named the Tomatis effect in his honor. Two other laws followed: if we supply the missing frequencies to the ear, the voice will immediately reflect this change; and we can restore hearing by retraining the muscles of the inner ear, when the loss is functional in nature. The Electronic Ear was devised to aid the ear in acquiring good listening, monitoring of language, and right ear dominance.

Dr. Tomatis was a tireless investigator and teacher, both in France at the French Ministry of employment, the French Air and Arsenal Ministry, the Paris School of Anthropology, and the Paris School of Practicing Psychologist, as well as abroad. He has written over fifteen books and received numerous distinctions: Knight of Public Health, 1951; Gold Medal for Scientific Research, 1958, in Brussels; Grande Medaille d'Or de la Cite de Paris, 1962; Prix Clemenceau Isaure, 1967; Medaille d'Or de la Societe Arts, Science et Lettres, 1967. He is also author of fourteen books and numerous articles in French and German on other subjects of interest to him: education, psychology, linguistics, and philosophy. He founded the International Society for Audio-Psycho-Phonology. A museum devoted entirely to his work was recently dedicated near Brussels. His work is currently available in an ever-growing number of countries worldwide.

Roberta Prada, contralto, is a graduate of Wellesley College and the Instituto Superior de Arte del Teatro Colon in Buenos Aires. She is trained and certified in the work of Dr. Tomatis and in neuro-linguistic programming. She is a principal in Vocal Images, a 501C3 corporation currently producing a documentary on the art of singing, and president of Vox Mentor LLC a company dedicated to projects aimed at furthering excellence in the arts.

Francis Keeping, baritone, specializes in the eighteenth century and bel canto periods. He is a principal in Vocal Images and in Vox Mentor LLC, producing documentaries and selling recordings and services to the music community. He teaches and coaches singers in vocal technique and style in New York City. With Ms. Prada he is revising and adapting the first translation into English of Jean Baptiste Faure's *La Voix et le Chant* for publication in the near future.

Pierre Sollier, licensed Marriage, Family and Child Counselor, received his M.A. in Clinical Psychology from the John F. Kennedy University. He trained directly with Dr. Tomatis and was founder of the Mozart Center in La Fayette, California. He is currently completing a book on the uses of Tomatis's techniques, titled *Listening for Wellness*, and lives in Oaxaca, Mexico.